Quick-Guides to Inclusion

Quick-Guides to Inclusion

Ideas for Educating Students with Disabilities

edited by

Michael F. Giangreco, Ph.D.
University of Vermont
Burlington

with contributions by

Barbara J. Ayres, Ph.D.
Chigee J. Cloninger, Ph.D.
Linda A. Davern, Ph.D.
Ruth E. Dennis, Ed.D., OTR
Mary Beth Doyle, Ph.D.
Susan W. Edelman, M.Ed., RPT
Deborah L. Hedeen, Ph.D.
Patricia A. Lee, Ed.D.

and

Patricia A. Prelock, Ph.D.

·P A U L·H·
BROOKES
PUBLISHING C°.

Baltimore • London • Toronto • Sydney

Paul H. Brookes Publishing Co.
Post Office Box 10624
Baltimore, Maryland 21285-0624

Typeset by Signature Typesetting & Design, Baltimore, Maryland.
Manufactured in the United States of America by
BookCrafters, Inc., Chelsea, Michigan.

Quick-Guide #1 is based on portions of the following article:
   Giangreco, M.F. (1996). What do I do now? A teacher's guide to including students with disabilities.
Educational Leadership, 53(5), 56–59.

Quick-Guide #2 is based on portions of the following article:
   Davern, L. (1996). Listening to parents of children with disabilities. *Educational Leadership*, 53(7),
61–63.

Quick-Guide #5 is based on portions of the following article:
   Ayres, B.J., & Hedeen, D.L. (1996). Been there, done that, didn't work: Alternative solutions for
behavior problems. *Educational Leadership*, 53(4), 48–50.

All royalties from the sale of this book are donated to nonprofit groups or agencies that meet human
needs.

The individuals and situations described in this book are completely fictional or are based on composites
of various people and circumstances, in which cases pseudonyms have been used. Any similarity to
actual individuals or circumstances is coincidental and no implications should be inferred.

Gender specifications used in this volume alternate throughout the text.

Library of Congress Cataloging-in-Publication Data

Quick-Guides to inclusion : ideas for educating students with disabilities / editor, Michael F. Giangreco ;
   with contributions by Barbara J. Ayres ... [et al.].
         p.   cm.
      Includes bibliographical references and index.
      ISBN 1-55766-303-3
      1. Inclusive education—United States.   2. Handicapped students—Education—United States.
   I. Giangreco, Michael F., 1956–   .   II. Ayres, Barbara.
   LC1201.Q53   1997
   371.9'046—dc20   97-7106
                                                                                              CIP

British Library Cataloguing in Publication data are available from the British Library.

Contents

Quick-Guide #1:   Including Students with Disabilities in the Classroom

1. Get a Little Help from Your Friends
2. Welcome the Student in Your Classroom
3. Be the Teacher for All the Students in Your Classroom
4. Make Sure All the Students Are Part of the Classroom Community
5. Establish Shared Expectations About the Student's Educational Program
6. Have Options for Including Students in Class Activities When Their Needs Vary
7. Provide Learning Experiences that Are Active and Participatory
8. Adapt Classroom Arrangements, Materials, and Strategies to Facilitate Effective Instruction
9. Make Sure Support Services Are Really Helping You Teach All the Students In Your Class
10. Evaluate the Effectiveness of Your Teaching

Quick-Guide #2:   Building Partnerships with Parents

1. Send a Clear and Consistent Message Regarding the Value of the Child
2. Put Yourself in the Shoes of the Parents
3. Demonstrate an Authentic Interest in Parents' Goals for Their Children
4. Use Everyday Language
5. Talk with Parents About How They Want to Share Information
6. Expand Your Awareness of Cultural Diversity
7. See Individuals—Challenge Stereotypes
8. Create Effective Forums for Planning and Problem Solving
9. Support Full Membership for All Children
10. Persevere in Building Partnerships with Parents

Quick-Guide #3:   Creating Partnerships with Paraprofessionals

1. Welcome the Paraprofessional to Your Classroom
2. Establish the Importance of the Paraprofessional as a Team Member

About the Editor

Michael F. Giangreco, Ph.D., Research Associate Professor, Department of Education, University Affiliated Program of Vermont, University of Vermont, 499C Waterman Building, Burlington, Vermont 05405-0160

Michael F. Giangreco has spent more than 20 years working with children and adults in a variety of capacities including special education teacher, community residence counselor, camp counselor, school administrator, educational consultant, university teacher, and researcher. Dr. Giangreco received a bachelor's degree from the State University of New York College at Buffalo and graduate degrees from the University of Vermont and the University of Virginia. He received his doctoral degree from Syracuse University and has been a faculty member at the University of Vermont since 1988.

His work and educational experiences have led Dr. Giangreco to focus his research, training, and other work activities on three interrelated aspects of educating students with and without disabilities in their local general education schools: 1) individualized curriculum planning, 2) adapting curriculum and instruction, and 3) coordinating support services in schools. Dr. Giangreco is the author of numerous professional publications, including *Choosing Options and Accommodations for Children (COACH): A Guide to Planning Inclusive Education* with Chigee J. Cloninger and Virginia Salce Iverson (Brookes Publishing Co., 1993) and *Vermont Interdependent Services Team Approach (VISTA): A Guide to Coordinating Educational Support Services* (Brookes Publishing Co., 1996), and is a frequent presenter of educational issues and strategies. Based at the College of Education and Social Services and the University Affiliated Program of Vermont, he has applied his work in numerous schools across North America. His work has been advanced by the feedback and input of innumerable students (with and without disabilities), parents, teachers, administrators, related services providers, and other colleagues.

Contributors

Barbara J. Ayres, Ph.D.
Assistant Professor
Department of Special Education and
    Reading
Montana State University
1500 North 30th Street
Billings, Montana 59101-0298

Chigee J. Cloninger, Ph.D.
Research Associate Professor
Department of Education
University Affiliated Program of Vermont
University of Vermont
499C Waterman Building
Burlington, Vermont 05405-0160

Linda A. Davern, Ph.D.
Assistant Professor
Department of Education
The Sage Colleges
45 Ferry Street
Troy, New York 12180

Ruth E. Dennis, Ed.D., OTR
Research Assistant Professor
Department of Education
University Affiliated Program of Vermont
University of Vermont
499C Waterman Building
Burlington, Vermont 05405-0160

Mary Beth Doyle, Ph.D.
Assistant Professor
Department of Education
Trinity College of Vermont
208 Colchester Avenue
Burlington, Vermont 05401

Susan W. Edelman, M.Ed., RPT
Lecturer
Department of Education
University Affiliated Program of Vermont
University of Vermont
499C Waterman Building
Burlington, Vermont 05405-0160

Deborah L. Hedeen, Ph.D.
Assistant Professor
Department of Special Education
Idaho State University
Box 8059
Pocatello, Idaho 83209

Patricia A. Lee, Ed.D.
Associate Professor
Department of Special Education
University of Northern Colorado
501 20th Street
Greeley, Colorado 80639

Patricia A. Prelock, Ph.D.
Research Associate Professor
Department of Education
University Affiliated Program of Vermont
University of Vermont
499C Waterman Building
Burlington, Vermont 05405-0160

What Are Quick-Guides and How Are They Used?

The Quick-Guides contained in this book are meant to provide relevant information that can be read in a short amount of time. So many of the teachers we encounter are anxious to get relevant information but find that they don't have enough time to read long articles and books.

Each of the five Quick-Guides contained in this volume follows a similar format. Therefore, you may consider each of the Quick-Guides as an individual document that can stand alone, even though the Quick-Guides are interrelated. Each Quick-Guide has

- A letter to the teacher that introduces the content
- A list of 10 Guidelines-at-a-Glance
- A set of the guidelines, each on a separate page, suitable for duplication as overhead transparencies
- A page of text discussing each of the 10 guidelines
- A short list of Selected References

The Quick-Guides are written for general education teachers, although they can be helpful to a variety of team members. You have permission to photocopy the Quick-Guides from this book to share with your colleagues. We thought this might be especially helpful for those of you who find yourself working with other general education teachers to facilitate the supported education of students with disabilities. As we shared these Quick-Guides prior to publication, we found they were frequently given to general educators by special education colleagues, were passed out to faculty members by their principals, and were used by staff development specialists and trainers as part of information packets. Some people used them to share information with parents, therapists, community members, school board members, student teachers, and college students.

We encourage you to share them with folks—that's the whole idea! If you have any ideas about future Quick-Guide topics, please feel free to contact me.

Good Luck!

Michael F. Giangreco

Quick-Guides to Inclusion

Quick-Guide #1

Including Students
with Disabilities
in the Classroom

Michael F. Giangreco

Quick-Guides to Inclusion:
Ideas for Educating Students with Disabilities

Michael F. Giangreco, Ph.D.
Series Editor

Dear Teacher,

You just found out that a student with disabilities is being placed in your classroom. I understand that you have lots of questions about what to do and how to do it. You probably know that there are countless resources to choose from to learn more about teaching a student with disabilities, but rumor has it you simply don't have time to read them all. Don't panic! My guess is that you probably already know much of what you need to for this to be a successful experience for you and your class; it's a matter of applying the knowledge and skills you already possess to a new situation. It's been done before by other teachers, and you can do it too. Most of what you need to do requires common sense-this isn't rocket science (but it is important!).

This Quick-Guide is designed to give you succinct information about some of the most important guidelines for successfully including students with disabilities. These guidelines are, of course, most effective when individualized in a thoughtful manner to match your own situation. I've listed 10 guidelines, each of which is followed by a brief explanation. Obviously, there is much more to learn than is presented in this short resource, so at the end of the Quick-Guide you'll find a list of "Selected References"; in the meantime this Quick-Guide will get you on your way.

Good Luck!

Michael

GUIDELINES-AT-A-GLANCE

1. Get a Little Help from Your Friends

2. Welcome the Student in Your Classroom

3. Be the Teacher for All the Students in Your Classroom

4. Make Sure All the Students Are Part of the Classroom Community

5. Establish Shared Expectations About the Student's Educational Program

6. Have Options for Including Students in Class Activities When Their Needs Vary

7. Provide Learning Experiences that Are Active and Participatory

8. Adapt Classroom Arrangements, Materials, and Strategies to Facilitate Effective Instruction

9. Make Sure Support Services Are Really Helping You Teach All the Students in Your Class

10. Evaluate the Effectiveness of Your Teaching

Quick-Guides to Inclusion: Ideas for Educating Students with Disabilities   ©Michael F. Giangreco
Available through Paul H. Brookes Publishing Co., Baltimore: 1-800-638-3775

#1

Get a Little Help
from Your Friends

Get a Little Help from Your Friends

There's lots to do, but no one expects you to do it all by yourself or know all the specialized information that can accompany a student with disabilities. Luckily, you're not alone. Most schools where students with disabilities are taught in general education classes develop a team to help plan and implement students' Individualized Education Programs—this is a good idea. Members frequently include the student and his parent(s), special education teachers, paraprofessionals, and support staff such as speech-language pathologists, physical therapists, and others. But make no mistake about it, general education teachers have much to contribute. Don't forget that you probably have 20–30 creative, energetic sources of ideas, inspiration, and assistance in your room all the time—your students can be your greatest resource if you let them.

Although collaborative teamwork is a crucial element of quality education, be on the lookout for good ideas run amuck. A common problem is that groups sometimes become unnecessarily large and unwieldy. Another problem can be an unhealthy compulsion to have too many meetings without a clear purpose and outcomes. These problems can complicate communication and decision making, overwhelm families, and inhibit constructive action. Beware of cheap imitations—just because there is a group, that doesn't mean it's a team. You'll know the impostor because its members often agree that each of the professional disciplines will have its own separate goals and agendas. In contrast, the real team shares a single set of educational goals that team members collectively pursue in a coordinated manner.

Quick-Guides to Inclusion: Ideas for Educating Students with Disabilities   ©Michael F. Giangreco
Available through Paul H. Brookes Publishing Co., Baltimore: 1-800-638-3775

#2

Welcome the Student
in Your Classroom

Quick-Guides to Inclusion: Ideas for Educating Students with Disabilities   ©Michael F. Giangreco
Available through Paul H. Brookes Publishing Co., Baltimore: 1-800-638-3775

Welcome the Student in Your Classroom

Welcoming the student with disabilities in your classroom may seem like a simple thing to do (and it is), but you might be surprised how frequently it doesn't happen. A common, yet devastating, experience for students with disabilities and their families is getting a message that the child is not welcome in the school or must "earn" the right to belong by meeting an arbitrary standard that invariably differs from school to school and state to state. It can be a difficult and unpleasant experience for a student with disabilities and her family to be actively or passively rejected by school personnel.

Beyond the effects on the student and family, what kind of message does your reaction to a student with disabilities send to others? As the classroom teacher, the students in your class look to you as their primary adult model during the school day. What do you want to model for your other students about similarities and differences, change, diversity, individuality, and caring? Whatever actions you choose to take or not take in terms of welcoming all your students can have powerful implications. There is no avoiding the fact that your colleagues at school will be watching too. My own experience is that, more often than not, it is the adults who have difficulty accepting the student with disabilities, not the children. By our providing a welcoming and accepting environment for all the children who live in our communities, a new generation is emerging who are more likely to have friends with disabilities in their classrooms, neighborhoods, and community activities, as a typical part of daily life.

So when a child with a disability comes to your classroom, welcome her as you would any other student. Talk to her, walk with her, encourage her, joke with her, and teach her. Let her know through your ongoing actions that she is an important member of your class.

Quick-Guides to Inclusion: Ideas for Educating Students with Disabilities   ©Michael F. Giangreco
Available through Paul H. Brookes Publishing Co., Baltimore: 1-800-638-3775

#3

Be the Teacher for All the Students in Your Classroom

Be the Teacher for All the Students in Your Classroom

When a student with disabilities is placed in a general education class, a common explicit or implicit understanding is that you, as the classroom teacher, are primarily a host rather than a teacher. Many teachers welcome this notion with open arms—it means someone else is responsible for the student with disabilities. This makes sense to many teachers, who already feel they have too much to do. There's just one catch: Merely hosting doesn't seem to work very well.

When the teacher serves as host, it's someone else, such as a paraprofessional, special educator, or another support person, who takes turns working with the student in the back of the classroom or in a different room. The teacher ends up having minimal interaction with this student and not having a good handle on what is going on. Many teachers say they don't really think of the student with disabilities as one of their students. I've heard teachers say, "I have 26 students plus John [a student with disabilities]. My job is to teach my 26 students and Karen's job [assistant] is to teach John." This perpetuates a lack of ownership and responsibility for the student's education and too often leaves major curricular and instructional decisions to hard-working but potentially under-qualified paraprofessionals.

Although you should expect to receive individually determined supports, I strongly encourage you to really be the teacher for all the students who are placed in your class. That means knowing what all your students are learning and personally spending time teaching each of them. Be flexible, but don't allow yourself to be relegated to being an "outsider" in your own classroom. If you are successful teaching students without disabilities, then you have the skills to be successful teaching students with disabilities.

Quick-Guides to Inclusion: Ideas for Educating Students with Disabilities ©Michael F. Giangreco
Available through Paul H. Brookes Publishing Co., Baltimore: 1-800-638-3775

#4

Make Sure All the Students Are Part of the Classroom Community

Make Sure All the Students
Are Part of the Classroom Community

In conjunction with welcoming the student with disabilities in your classroom and establishing yourself as his teacher, it's important to have the student be a valued member of the classroom community. Where students spend time, what they do, when, and with whom play major roles in defining affiliation and status within the classroom. Too many students with disabilities are "placed" in the general education class but are not included much of the time. They spend a significant amount of time apart from their classmates, do different activities, and have a different daily schedule from their peers. This inhibits learning with and from peers (who can be great teachers) and often leads to social isolation.

It is all too common to find the student with a disability seated on the fringe of the class. Make sure this student has the same kind of desk as his classmates and is seated with them, rather than apart from them. If the desks are arranged in groups of four, make sure he is in a group with three other students. Students with disabilities have to be physically present to be part of what's happening.

Make sure that the student with disability participates in the same activities as his classmates as much as possible (even though his goals may be different from those of other classmates). If everyone in the class writes in a journal, so should this student (even if it requires adaptation to a nonwritten form). If all the students do homework, so should this student, at an appropriate level. If all the students are doing a science experiment, so should this student. Although some individualization may be necessary, the student's daily schedule should allow ample opportunities to learn, socialize, play, hang out, and work with the rest of the class.

Quick-Guides to Inclusion: Ideas for Educating Students with Disabilities   ©Michael F. Giangreco
Available through Paul H. Brookes Publishing Co., Baltimore: 1-800-638-3775

#5

Establish Shared Expectations About the Student's Educational Program

---

One of the most common sources of anxiety for classroom teachers is understanding what others, such as parents, administrators, and special educators, expect them to teach. "Do you expect me to teach this student most or all of what the other students without disabilities are learning?" Sometimes the answer will be "Yes," sometimes "No." A crucial step is to make sure that team members share a common expectation of what the student should learn in the class and who will be doing the teaching.

Start by having the team identify a small set of the student's highest learning priorities. Next, have the team agree on a larger set of additional learning outcomes that reflect a broad-based educational program. These additional learning outcomes should clarify what parts of the general education curriculum the student will be expected to pursue and may include learning outcomes that are not typically part of the general program. Many students with disabilities also need to be provided with supports that allow for their participation in class. These supports should be identified and distinguished from learning outcomes. When supports are inadvertently identified as goals or objectives, it can lead to an unnecessarily passive educational program for the student with disabilities.

It can be helpful to summarize these three categories of the educational program—1) priorities, 2) other learning outcomes, and 3) supports—on a one- or two-page "Program-at-a-Glance." This type of concise listing of learning outcomes and supports can assist in planning and scheduling, serve as a helpful reminder of the student's individualized needs, and provide an effective way to communicate student needs to special area teachers such as art, music, and physical education teachers. By clarifying what the team expects the student to learn, the stage is set for a productive school year.

Quick-Guides to Inclusion: Ideas for Educating Students with Disabilities   ©Michael F. Giangreco
Available through Paul H. Brookes Publishing Co., Baltimore: 1-800-638-3775

#6

Have Options for Including Students in Class Activities When Their Needs Vary

---

Have Options for Including Students in Class Activities When Their Needs Vary

When a student with disabilities is placed in a class where some of her educational needs differ from those of the majority of the class, teachers often question the appropriateness of the placement. "Why is the student being placed in my sixth-grade class when she is functioning at a much earlier level?" You don't have to be at "grade level" to have a successful educational experience in any particular grade. In fact, many schools are purposely developing multigrade classrooms where teachers successfully accommodate students with a wide range of abilities in the same class.

It is important to have options for including a student with disabilities in class activities when some or many of her needs differ from those of other class members. The easiest option exists when the learning outcomes for the student with disabilities are the same as those for the rest of the class. In such cases the student may or may not require instructional accommodations to successfully participate in class activities. A second option exists when the student participates in class activities while pursuing learning outcomes in the same curriculum area as the rest of the class but at a different level, such as different vocabulary words, math problems, or science concepts. A third option exists when the student with disabilities participates in class activities while pursuing individually determined learning outcomes from curriculum areas different from those of the rest of the class. For example, the student could be learning communication, literacy, or socialization skills in a science activity where the focus for the rest of the class is science learning outcomes. There also may be occasions where the student with disability requires an alternative learning experience that is not part of a class activity.

Quick-Guides to Inclusion: Ideas for Educating Students with Disabilities   ©Michael F. Giangreco
Available through Paul H. Brookes Publishing Co., Baltimore: 1-800-638-3775

#7

Provide Learning Experiences that Are Active and Participatory

---

Provide Learning Experiences
that Are Active and Participatory

I've heard teachers say, "A student with disabilities wouldn't get a lot out of being in that class because the teacher does a lot of large-group lectures, worksheets, and paper-and-pencil tests." My first reaction is, "You're right, it doesn't sound like that situation matches the needs of the student with disabilities." This leaves me wondering, "Is this kind of educational situation a mismatch for any of the students who don't have disability labels?" Given the diversity of learning styles among students, educators are increasingly questioning whether passive, didactic approaches really meet the needs of very many students.

Activity-based learning is well suited to including learners with a wide range of educational needs and learning styles. One of the gifts that students with disabilities can bring to the classroom is to highlight the need to use more active, participatory, creative approaches to learning. In the process of increasing the amount of activity and participation to accommodate the needs of a student with disabilities, teachers often realize that these approaches are motivating, preferred, and effective for many other students in the class. They seem to be more enjoyable for the teachers too.

Increasing activity and participation can include a wide range of options, such as individual or cooperative projects, drama, experiments, field study, art media, computers, research, educational games, multimedia, various forms of choral responding, and many others. Any actions you take as a teacher can probably be adapted to be a meaningful learning experience for your students. Making sure students have lots to do that is interesting and motivating can have side benefits such as diminishing behavior problems and encouraging positive social behaviors. Your students can be very helpful in designing active learning experiences.

Quick-Guides to Inclusion: Ideas for Educating Students with Disabilities   ©Michael F. Giangreco
Available through Paul H. Brookes Publishing Co., Baltimore: 1-800-638-3775

#8

Adapt Classroom Arrangements, Materials, and Strategies to Facilitate Effective Instruction

---

Adapt Classroom Arrangements, Materials, and Strategies to Facilitate Effective Instruction

When placing students with disabilities in general education classes it is important to ensure that the instruction they receive is effective in meeting their individual needs. Often, when teaching students with disabilities, we need to be more precise and deliberate in how we teach. Even if the content of instruction is meaningful and at an appropriate level of difficulty, it's not enough; we still have to provide effective instruction.

Providing effective instruction to students with disabilities within large groups, in small groups, or individually often requires that instruction be adapted. This can mean adapting the instructional arrangement to facilitate learning opportunities, proximity to peers, or access to competent modeling. Sometimes that adaptation can be as basic as considering a different way for a student to respond if he has difficulty using typical modes like speaking or writing.

Adapting teaching methods should also be considered. For example, if group lecture doesn't seem to be working, consider alternatives (e.g., cooperative groups, computer-assisted instruction, guided practice). Materials can also be adapted to match the student's characteristics or interests. For example, adding tactile or auditory cues for a student with visual impairments, making something bigger or easier to manipulate for a student with physical disabilities, or accounting for a student's interests when adapting materials may increase the motivation of a student who is easily bored or distracted. Rely on the whole team and class to assist with adaptation ideas.

Quick-Guides to Inclusion: Ideas for Educating Students with Disabilities   ©Michael F. Giangreco
Available through Paul H. Brookes Publishing Co., Baltimore: 1-800-638-3775

#9

Make Sure
Support Services Are
Really Helping You Teach All
the Students in Your Class

Make Sure Support Services Are Really Helping You Teach All the Students in Your Class

It's important to find out what types of supports are available to assist students in your class. While you are undoubtedly familiar with how to obtain many commonly available support services, the special education teacher in your school often is knowledgeable about other supports.

Having many support service personnel involved with students can be a help or a hindrance; it comes down to how the individual works with you to support the class. In the best case scenario, you will work with support personnel who are competent and collaborative. These folks will take care to ensure that what they *do* helps you teach your students more effectively. They will *do* this by getting to know the students and routines of your classroom as well as understanding your ideas and concerns. Their collaboration with you will take into account potential disruptions to your classroom, the impact on students' social relationships, and components of the educational program your team previously determined.

You can advocate for yourself and your students by becoming an informed consumer of support services. Learn to ask good questions. Be assertive if you feel you are being asked to do something that doesn't make sense to you. Be as explicit as you can about what type of support you need. Sometimes you may need specific information or materials or someone to demonstrate a technique. At other times, the need may be for someone with whom you can exchange ideas or just get some validation that you are headed in the right direction. When you are on the receiving end of appropriately provided support services, you will feel like you have been helped, not hindered.

Quick-Guides to Inclusion: Ideas for Educating Students with Disabilities   ©Michael F. Giangreco
Available through Paul H. Brookes Publishing Co., Baltimore: 1-800-638-3775

#10

Evaluate the Effectiveness of Your Teaching

Quick-Guides to Inclusion: Ideas for Educating Students with Disabilities   ©Michael F. Giangreco
Available through Paul H. Brookes Publishing Co., Baltimore: 1-800-638-3775

Evaluate the Effectiveness of Your Teaching

Evaluating the effectiveness of one's own teaching is important for adjusting and improving future instruction. We commonly evaluate our teaching through the achievements of our students. To determine the extent and quality of learning for a student with disabilities, the team initially must have done a good job of determining important and appropriate learning outcomes. Although evaluation for students with disabilities may take some of the same forms as it does for other students (e.g., written tests, reports, projects), some students with disabilities will need alternative testing accommodations. In addition, portfolio assessments that have become popular in general education can be adapted for use with students with disabilities.

Often we assume that if students without disabilities get "good grades," this will translate into future life success in education, employment, and opportunities. Although differing for each student, this assumption can be very dangerous to make when discussing the future of students with disabilities. Traditional forms of school testing and evaluation may provide certain types of information, but they are insufficient for evaluating the impact of our teaching. Unfortunately, we have far too many graduates with disabilities whose postschool lives are marked by unemployment, health problems, loneliness, or isolation from community life—despite the fact that their progress reports were glowing. Therefore, we need to continually evaluate whether a student's achievement is being applied to real life as evidenced by her physical and emotional health; her positive social relationships; and her abilities to communicate, self-advocate, make informed choices, demonstrate personal growth, and increasingly access places and activities that are personally meaningful. In so doing, we can strive to ensure that our teaching will really make a positive difference in our students' lives.

Quick-Guides to Inclusion: Ideas for Educating Students with Disabilities   ©Michael F. Giangreco
Available through Paul H. Brookes Publishing Co., Baltimore: 1-800-638-3775

Dennis, R., Williams, W., Giangreco, M.F., & Cloninger, C. (1993). Quality of life as context for planning and evaluation of services for people with disabilities. *Exceptional Children, 59*, 499–512.

Giangreco, M.F. (1996). *Vermont interdependent services team approach (VISTA): A guide to coordinating educational support services.* Baltimore: Paul H. Brookes Publishing Co.

Giangreco, M.F., Cloninger, C.J., Dennis, R., & Edelman, S. (1994). Problem-solving methods to facilitate inclusive education. In J.S. Thousand, R.A. Villa, & A.I. Nevin (Eds.), *Creativity and collaborative learning: A practical guide to empowering students and teachers* (pp. 321–346). Baltimore: Paul H. Brookes Publishing Co.

Giangreco, M.F., Cloninger, C.J., & Iverson, V.S. (1993). *Choosing option and accommodations for children (COACH): A guide to planning inclusive education.* Baltimore: Paul H. Brookes Publishing Co.

Giangreco, M.F., Dennis, R., Cloninger, C., Edelman, S., & Schattman, R. (1993). "I've counted Jon": Transformational experiences of teachers educating students with disabilities. *Exceptional Children, 59*, 359–372.

Harmin, M. (1994). *Inspiring active learning: A handbook for teachers.* Alexandria, VA: Association for Supervision and Curriculum Development.

Stainback, S., & Stainback, W. (Eds.). (1992). *Curriculum considerations in inclusive classrooms: Facilitating learning for all students.* Baltimore: Paul H. Brookes Publishing Co.

Stainback, S., & Stainback, W. (Eds.). (1996). *Inclusion: A guide for educators.* Baltimore: Paul H. Brookes Publishing Co.

Villa, R., & Thousand, J. (Eds.). (1996). *Creating an inclusive school.* Alexandria, VA: Association for Supervision and Curriculum Development.

Quick-Guide #2

Building Partnerships
with Parents

Linda A. Davern

Quick-Guides to Inclusion:
Ideas for Educating Students with Disabilities

Michael F. Giangreco, Ph.D.
Series Editor

Quick-Guides to Inclusion: Ideas for Educating Students with Disabilities   ©Michael F. Giangreco
Available through Paul H. Brookes Publishing Co., Baltimore: 1-800-638-3775

Dear Teacher,

What can teaching teams do to build productive alliances or strengthen existing relationships with the parents or caregivers of children with disabilities? With this question in mind, I conducted interviews with families whose children with disabilities were included in general education classrooms. Many of these children needed support and modifications to participate successfully in class activities. These parents offered suggestions for how the quality of relationships between school personnel and families could be improved. The following guidelines are based on their perspectives.

Building successful partnerships with parents is a goal for effective teachers as each school year commences. The approaches these parents suggest can assist teachers and other school staff in ensuring that they are successful with a broader range of parents. Through showing interest in the uniqueness of the child, attempting to understand the parent's frame of reference, engaging in effective communication skills, growing in awareness of cultural diversity, creating productive forums for group problem solving, and showing perseverance, teachers can more successfully join with parents in the common mission of educating children. Each of the guidelines presented here is followed by a brief discussion. At the end you'll find a list of "Selected References" if you wish to pursue more in-depth information; in the meantime this Quick-Guide will get you started.

Good Luck!

Linda

GUIDELINES-AT-A-GLANCE

1. Send a Clear and Consistent Message Regarding the Value of the Child

2. Put Yourself in the Shoes of the Parents

3. Demonstrate an Authentic Interest in Parents' Goals for Their Children

4. Use Everyday Language

5. Talk with Parents About How They Want to Share Information

6. Expand Your Awareness of Cultural Diversity

7. See Individuals—Challenge Stereotypes

8. Create Effective Forums for Planning and Problem Solving

9. Support Full Membership for All Children

10. Persevere in Building Partnerships with Parents

Quick-Guides to Inclusion: Ideas for Educating Students with Disabilities   ©Michael F. Giangreco
Available through Paul H. Brookes Publishing Co., Baltimore: 1-800-638-3775

#1

Send a Clear and Consistent Message Regarding the Value of the Child

---

Send a Clear and Consistent Message Regarding the Value of the Child

The ways in which school personnel talk about children in both formal and informal interactions early in the school year have a significant impact on the development of relationships with families. The ability to see appealing aspects of a child's personality, aside from the arena of academic achievement, is important to many parents. As one mother, Gail, put it,

> for teachers to say to me, "I really like your kid," or "You know, he really has a great sense of humor"...that really lets me know a couple of things—...that they really care about him as a person and see him as a person.

Conveying excitement and optimism about the child is an ability that is greatly valued by many parents. Many parents appreciate personnel who are able to focus on their individual child's progress as opposed to constantly using other children as a point of reference for comparison.

Additional characteristics that indicate to some parents that personnel value and accept their children include: 1) a willingness to listen to the child, 2) not engaging in interactions that are demeaning to the child (e.g., talking about the child in his presence), and 3) talking respectfully to the child. As Anna, another parent, put it, "Just take her for who she is... So she's not going to be the top of her class in gym. We understand that. Just take her for who she is. Find space for her." Building a foundation of good feeling starts with staff conveying consistent messages that they see the child as an interesting individual, are happy to have the child in class, and hold high expectations for what that child will achieve.

Quick-Guides to Inclusion: Ideas for Educating Students with Disabilities   ©Michael F. Giangreco
Available through Paul H. Brookes Publishing Co., Baltimore: 1-800-638-3775

#2

Put Yourself in the Shoes of the Parents

Put Yourself in the Shoes of the Parents

Parents are unlikely to ever completely understand the life of the teacher, and, likewise, most teachers will not fully appreciate the day-to-day experiences of the parent who has a child with a disability. Parents told us that they recognized and appreciated the effort put forth by school personnel to understand what it is like to have a child with a disability—what it is like to negotiate with both the general and special education bureaucracies in order to gain access to classes, accommodations, and support services for their child.

For many of the parents, advocacy was necessary to achieve what they viewed as a decent education for their children. They felt there was no alternative to fighting. Parents felt they were often viewed as impatient, and they wanted staff to better understand their frustrations with the pace of change. Whether the change was in the areas of building friendships, developing adaptations, or developing effective planning teams, some parents felt they couldn't afford to accept a slow rate of progress.

As one parent put it, "You gotta understand; we don't have time....My daughter is getting older every year....I haven't got a lot of time." School staff who attempt to understand the parents' frame of reference are less likely to develop judgmental attitudes so damaging to the home—school relationship.

Quick-Guides to Inclusion: Ideas for Educating Students with Disabilities   ©Michael F. Giangreco
Available through Paul H. Brookes Publishing Co., Baltimore: 1-800-638-3775

#3

Demonstrate an Authentic Interest in Parents' Goals for Their Children

---

Demonstrate an Authentic Interest in Parents' Goals for Their Children

School staff need to demonstrate an interest in what the parents see as meaningful goals for their child. A first step in creating this dialogue is establishing a rapport with individual parents. Angela spoke repeatedly about a teacher her son had the previous year.

> She's just the type of person…big smile…very warm and very assertive…. Maybe I might be a little bit nervous the first meeting—and she answered questions I would have [asked] before I could even ask them. She makes me feel comfortable. Her first priority is not only with the child, but with the parent.

Parents view some staff as very skilled in lessening the psychological distance between parents and professionals. These teachers are able to create an atmosphere where parents do not feel that they have to "watch their P's and Q's," as one parent put it. School staff do this through their choice of language, as well as their interaction styles. Teachers' interest in parents' ideas can be important to the families with whom they are working.

Parents also discussed a considerable number of interactions as evidence of an "expert kind of syndrome." Some parents got the feeling that the attitude coming from staff was, "You couldn't possibly know what you're talking about." One parent described a critical distinction between those personnel who talk **with** parents and those who talk **at** them.

Teachers **can** maintain their expertise as educators while fully acknowledging the information and insights held by parents. The interplay of these complementary roles can greatly enrich the outcome for students.

Quick-Guides to Inclusion: Ideas for Educating Students with Disabilities   ©Michael F. Giangreco
Available through Paul H. Brookes Publishing Co., Baltimore: 1-800-638-3775

#4

Use Everyday Language

Quick-Guides to Inclusion: Ideas for Educating Students with Disabilities   ©Michael F. Giangreco
Available through Paul H. Brookes Publishing Co., Baltimore: 1-800-638-3775

Use Everyday Language

Parents can feel excluded from the educational planning process when professionals use educational terms that are unclear to the parents. One parent referred to this practice as "blowing all that smoke." Jargon is frequently used in relation to test results, staffing patterns, and ways of organizing and identifying services. For example, it would not be unusual to hear a statement like this one during a planning team meeting: "He's currently in a 12-1-1 and could move to consult if the one-to-one follows along. Could the O.T. do push-in in that setting? His fine motor skills need a lot of work." Although a person who is a member of the school community may be able to make sense of this statement, a parent is often left guessing. As another parent put it,

> You know, that's a *riot* when they start talking "parallel curriculum." When you do that stuff you just close out the parent—as soon as you use language that's exclusive of the parent—they're gone. You have to get rid of the jargon.

It is an unfortunate irony that, in order to graduate from many teacher preparation programs, preservice teachers must master a professional language that ultimately creates significant barriers in being effective in their interactions with the families they are meant to serve. Perceptive teachers recognize the distance that is created by the use of professional jargon, minimize its use, and explain commonly used professional terms.

Quick-Guides to Inclusion: Ideas for Educating Students with Disabilities ©Michael F. Giangreco
Available through Paul H. Brookes Publishing Co., Baltimore: 1-800-638-3775

#5

Talk with Parents About How They Want to Share Information

Talk with Parents About How They Want to Share Information

Successful collaboration requires effective ongoing communication between home and school. Some parents thought that having one person as the primary contact would be helpful, yet several parents did not want to have a person affiliated with special education as their primary contact for fear that this would lessen the feelings of ownership on the part of the general educator for the child's progress. This dilemma results from the interplay between two systems. Many of these parents have struggled over a period of years to create a place for their child within the "general" education structure. When the primary contact with school is a representative of the separate structure, the membership can feel tenuous. Parents wanted their child to be viewed as "just one of the kids." Any practice that seemed to place more ownership and responsibility for the child's success on the special educator (or sometimes a related services provider) was, for the most part, unsettling for these parents. However, consistent communication with a person who really knew the child was important, as well.

Schools will need to discuss with parents how they would like to communicate, with whom they would like to communicate, and what frequency of communication can be feasibly arranged with specific members of the team. Personnel will need to understand that parents' preferences for involvement may change over time given a variety of factors, such as the child's age and the family's circumstances.

#6

Expand Your Awareness of Cultural Diversity

Quick-Guides to Inclusion: Ideas for Educating Students with Disabilities   ©Michael F. Giangreco
Available through Paul H. Brookes Publishing Co., Baltimore: 1-800-638-3775

Building on awareness of cultural diversity will strengthen school personnel's ability to teach as well as interact successfully with families. Marguerite, a parent, shared her observations:

> I think a lot of the teachers have never been in contact with minority children, or have had any training in multiculturalism or diversity, or know anything about these children or their cultural backgrounds and their lives, and then they are making assessments of these children based on *their* values and I think it's wrong.

Schools that are working toward multiculturalism provide diversity-related learning experiences for staff and also ensure that children see representation of their ethnicity in personnel as well as curriculum and materials. In addition, the emphasis on varied styles of learning that accompanies a multicultural approach lessens the likelihood of special education referral for some children.

Through effective staff development, schools can assist personnel in examining "the cultural base of their own belief system" in relation to children and families (Harry, 1992, p. 23) and how these beliefs have an impact on relationships. Culture must be addressed in all its complexity, emphasizing that "cultures are fluid and are greatly influenced by acculturation, generational status, gender, social class, education, occupational group and numerous other variables" (Harry et al., 1995, p. 106). Such an approach will ensure that personnel are aware of the cultural lenses through which they make judgments about children and families.

Quick-Guides to Inclusion: Ideas for Educating Students with Disabilities ©Michael F. Giangreco
Available through Paul H. Brookes Publishing Co., Baltimore: 1-800-638-3775

#7

See Individuals—
Challenge Stereotypes

See Individuals—Challenge Stereotypes

Some parents express concerns about assumptions they felt were made about them and their parenting skills simply because their child had a disability. One mother, Doria, saw some of these attitudes arising from a lack of understanding of some types of disabilities, such as emotional disturbance:

> I didn't think [teachers have] had enough training to realize that this child had a particular problem...they just see it as a child coming from a home that wasn't properly fit or something...they were trying to blame it on the parent.

Another parent, Marguerite, felt that school personnel frequently "lumped parents together"—working from inaccurate assumptions about single parents and parents who were not of European heritage: All single parents are dysfunctional, all minority parents are—that's a crock."

School personnel need opportunities to explore the impulse to stereotype. This can be accomplished through carefully designed staff development efforts that explore the inaccurate generalizations that sometimes emerge in our interaction patterns. Personnel can also find ways to take individual initiative by offering examples from their own experiences that contradict the stereotypes expressed by others.

Quick-Guides to Inclusion: Ideas for Educating Students with Disabilities   ©Michael F. Giangreco
Available through Paul H. Brookes Publishing Co., Baltimore: 1-800-638-3775

#8

Create Effective
Forums for Planning
and Problem Solving

Create Effective Forums for Planning and Problem Solving

Yearly meetings, mandated by law, are held for each child with an Individualized Education Program. During these meetings, assessments are reviewed, individual goals are identified, placement decisions are made, and support services are determined. Some of the most difficult interactions parents experience are at these meetings. It is not unusual for parents to describe these meetings as "very, very intimidating." Parents I spoke with often felt that their ideas were rarely being sought in a meaningful way.

In contrast, some teams hold meetings not just yearly, but on an ongoing basis. The key people involved with a child (e.g., teachers, parents, related services providers, classroom assistants) meet regularly throughout the year. These meetings provide a context and opportunity for coherent planning for a child. This includes sharing successful teaching strategies, discussing student progress, identifying the next year's teacher early in the current school year, and ensuring that important information is shared year to year. Although problems may be discussed at these meetings, they are not the sole focus. Opportunities existed to discuss achievement, friendships, interesting stories, or humorous anecdotes. As one mother put it, "When we go to team meetings, a lot of times it is a celebration. That's how it feels. By George, we're doing something right here; it's working!"

Districts need to develop expertise in the area of team planning for individual children (Giangreco, 1996; Giangreco, Cloninger, & Iverson, 1993; Thousand & Villa, 1992). At least one parent who had initiated such meetings could see how a similar model had utility for a number of children throughout the school whose situations required key adults to do some intensive planning on a short- or long-term basis.

#9

Support Full Membership
for All Children

Quick-Guides to Inclusion: Ideas for Educating Students with Disabilities   ©Michael F. Giangreco
Available through Paul H. Brookes Publishing Co., Baltimore: 1-800-638-3775

Support Full Membership for All Children

Parents often have to advocate extensively in order to gain a general class placement for their child. Too often, such placements are the result of their efforts as opposed to a policy or initiative by the school. Schools will not become proficient in building alliances with these families until general class membership, with adequate supports, is the norm for children with disabilities. It is crucial for districts to develop long-term, schoolwide plans to offer full membership to all students, as opposed to setting up programs for children only in response to the requests of individual parents (Gartner & Lipsky, 1987; Stainback & Stainback, 1990). Teachers can actively support such restructuring (with appropriate safeguards to ensure adequate resources). This can be done by joining community organizations whose goals are related to building inclusive schools, uniting with other staff and parents who have similar goals and interests related to inclusive practices, and initiating and serving on school restructuring work groups. As a result of the action plans that evolve from such efforts, inclusive settings will be available to those children whose parents are not in a position, for various reasons, to undertake extensive advocacy on behalf of their children.

Quick-Guides to Inclusion: Ideas for Educating Students with Disabilities ©Michael F. Giangreco
Available through Paul H. Brookes Publishing Co., Baltimore: 1-800-638-3775

#10

Persevere in Building Partnerships with Parents

Quick-Guides to Inclusion: Ideas for Educating Students with Disabilities   ©Michael F. Giangreco
Available through Paul H. Brookes Publishing Co., Baltimore: 1-800-638-3775

Although school teams are required by federal law to invite parents into the planning process for their children with disabilities, the collaborative outcome envisioned by the legislation does not always materialize. Perseverance in attempting to form partnerships with parents is a posture that many parents feel is critical. Many parents with whom I spoke thought that schools gave up too quickly and that some personnel were quick to dismiss parents who didn't attend meetings. These parents felt that building partnerships took commitment and vision over the long-term and that the degree of parent participation, for many families, was a direct result of school practices. They suggested looking at how schools share information with parents, how schools can demonstrate more flexibility in setting up meeting times with parents, and ways to assist parents in connecting with each other in order to provide assistance, such as alternating child care to free each other to attend planning meetings. As one parent put it, school personnel need to "make it happen," that is, to extend themselves and do what needs to be done to build partnerships with parents.

As stated by a father, once a district begins to work in a different way with families, it might take time, but the word gets around:

> Once you make that decision to team [with parents]—the first year that you do it, maybe you're not going to get all the parents, but parents know each other, and give it a little time, nurture it along, and you get a parent saying, "This new thing—there's a lot more sharing there. It's better."

Quick-Guides to Inclusion: Ideas for Educating Students with Disabilities   ©Michael F. Giangreco
Available through Paul H. Brookes Publishing Co., Baltimore: 1-800-638-3775

Selected References

Davern, L. (1994). Parents' perspectives on relationships with professionals in inclusive educational settings. *Dissertation Abstracts International, 56,* 9522518.

Gartner, A., & Lipsky, D. (1987). Beyond special education: Toward a quality system for all students. *Harvard Educational Review, 57*(4), 367–395.

Giangreco, M.F. (1996). *Vermont interdependent services team approach (VISTA): A guide to coordinating educational support services.* Baltimore: Paul H. Brookes Publishing Co.

Giangreco, M.F., Cloninger, C.J., & Iverson, V.S. (1993). *Choosing options and accommodations for children (COACH): A guide to planning inclusive education.* Baltimore: Paul H. Brookes Publishing Co.

Harry, B. (1992). *Cultural diversity, families, and the special education system.* New York: Teachers College Press.

Harry, B., Grenot-Scheyer, M., Smith-Lewis, M., Park, H., Xin, F., & Schwartz, I. (1995). Developing culturally inclusive services or individuals with severe disabilities. *Journal of The Association for Persons with Severe Handicaps, 20*(2), 99–109.

Stainback, S., & Stainback, W. (1990). Inclusive schooling. In W. Stainback & S. Stainback (Eds.), *Support networks for inclusive schooling: Interdependent integrated education* (pp. 3–23). Baltimore: Paul H. Brookes Publishing Co.

Thousand, J. S., & Villa, R.A. (1992). Collaborative teams: A powerful tool in school restructuring. In R. A. Villa, J. S. Thousand, W. Stainback, & S. Stainback (Eds.), *Restructuring for caring and effective education: An administrative guide to creating heterogeneous schools* (pp. 61–72). Baltimore: Paul H. Brookes Publishing Co.

Quick-Guide #3

Creating Partnerships with Paraprofessionals

Mary Beth Doyle and Patricia A. Lee

Quick-Guides to Inclusion:
Ideas for Educating Students with Disabilities

Michael F. Giangreco, Ph.D.
Series Editor

Quick-Guides to Inclusion: Ideas for Educating Students with Disabilities   ©Michael F. Giangreco
Available through Paul H. Brookes Publishing Co., Baltimore: 1-800-638-3775

Dear Teacher,

Sometimes when a student with disabilities is placed in your classroom, a paraprofessional is assigned to help you support that student, as well as the rest of the students in the classroom community. It is a different experience sharing your classroom with another adult—we hope a positive one. Unfortunately, if your experience is similar to that of many classroom teachers, you probably will not receive information about how to incorporate another adult into your classroom in a manner that will maximize the teaching and learning opportunities for all of the students in your classroom.

The 10 guidelines included in this Quick-Guide are intended to enhance the partnership between general educators and paraprofessionals, so that together you can meet the needs of students with all types of characteristics in the context of the general education classroom. Each guideline is followed by a brief description, and a list of "Selected References" is included at the end if you are interested in more in-depth information. Enjoy this opportunity to get to know the paraprofessional who will be a member of your instructional team this school year.

Good Luck!

Mary Beth and Patricia

GUIDELINES-AT-A-GLANCE

1. Welcome the Paraprofessional to Your Classroom

2. Establish the Importance of the Paraprofessional as a Team Member

3. Clarify the Paraprofessional's Roles and Responsibilities

4. Establish Shared Expectations for Student Learning and Classroom Management

5. Ensure that the Paraprofessional Is Guided by Certified Staff

6. Review Paraprofessional Activities Regularly

7. Establish Procedures for Unexpected Situations

8. Ensure that Paraprofessionals Promote Student Responsibility

9. Establish Times and Ways to Communicate

10. Evaluate the Effectiveness of the Paraprofessional

Quick-Guides to Inclusion: Ideas for Educating Students with Disabilities   ©Michael F. Giangreco
Available through Paul H. Brookes Publishing Co., Baltimore: 1-800-638-3775

#1

Welcome the Paraprofessional to Your Classroom

Welcome the Paraprofessional to Your Classroom

Think about how you would like to be welcomed to a new setting and do those simple, yet important, things for the paraprofessional. Prepare a place for her (e.g., desk, table, mailbox, materials, coffee cup). Introduce her to others on the faculty and staff. Give her a tour around the school, highlighting those places you and your students frequent (e.g., faculty room, library, art room). Model for the students that the two of you are a team. Demonstrate respect by asking the paraprofessional's opinion on classroom decisions (e.g., student arrangement, learning centers, student work displays).

Perhaps the most important thing you can do every day is to thank the paraprofessional for her effort and contributions. Tell her that you appreciate her ideas and support. Remember her on special occasions (e.g., birthday, holidays); these gestures of appreciation do make a difference.

Through our experiences, we have learned that, if these things do not occur, paraprofessionals may end up working in isolation within the classroom. In such situations, paraprofessionals tend to work exclusively with the student with disabilities, rather than with all of the students in the class. As a result, both the student and the paraprofessional can become separated from the rest of the class even though they may share the same physical space of the general education classroom.

When paraprofessionals are welcomed, feel like they are an important part of the classroom, and have a place in the classroom, the foundation is laid for a productive partnership. Together, you and the paraprofessional can create a caring classroom community where all children are welcomed and supported in making progress toward their individualized learning goals.

Quick-Guides to Inclusion: Ideas for Educating Students with Disabilities   ©Michael F. Giangreco
Available through Paul H. Brookes Publishing Co., Baltimore: 1-800-638-3775

#2

Establish the Importance
of the Paraprofessional
as a Team Member

Establish the Importance of the Paraprofessional as a Team Member

In most schools there are several types of "teams" (e.g., grade-level teams, content area teams, student support teams). Each team consists of a variety of people (e.g., students, parents, paraprofessionals, teachers, related services personnel) and has different, though interrelated purposes. Start by identifying the teams on which the paraprofessional needs to be an active member. Invite the paraprofessional accordingly and establish the reasons for his involvement.

Once the paraprofessional is involved with the team, there are several things that you can do to maximize the probability that his involvement will be substantive. Prior to team meetings, make sure the paraprofessional knows the purpose of the meeting, has an agenda, and knows how to get items added to the agenda. Suggest ways that he can prepare for meetings in advance. As the meeting starts, introduce him to other team members. Explain that you and the paraprofessional work together to meet the needs of all of the students in the classroom. Ask for his opinions, observations, questions, and comments. Like other team members, the paraprofessional may have tasks to complete as a result of the meeting. Check to see that the tasks are in alignment with his role as a paraprofessional.

In situations where the importance of the paraprofessional is not established, there is a diminished motivation for the paraprofessional to contribute and his work may become isolated and routinized. As a result, the paraprofessional can become less apt to offer creative ideas, suggestions, and important feedback. The whole team suffers if they neglect this significant resource. As the teacher, demonstrate that the paraprofessional is a valued and respected team member; we hope others will follow suit.

Quick-Guides to Inclusion: Ideas for Educating Students with Disabilities   ©Michael F. Giangreco
Available through Paul H. Brookes Publishing Co., Baltimore: 1-800-638-3775

#3

Clarify the
Paraprofessional's
Roles and Responsibilities

Clarify the Paraprofessional's Roles and Responsibilities

It is not uncommon for classroom teachers and paraprofessionals to experience some initial confusion about roles and responsibilities; there are many ways to avoid this problem. Think about your own role as the classroom teacher and make a list of your responsibilities. Ask the paraprofessional to do the same. Discuss these lists with each other with the intent of clarifying both of your roles and associated responsibilities. Make this conversation an ongoing, dynamic one as your roles and responsibilities grow and change throughout the year. The cumulative effects of such conversations can lead to increased clarity about the roles and responsibilities of the paraprofessional in relation to yours as the classroom teacher.

It has been our experience that, when there is a lack of clarity about the paraprofessional's roles and subsequent responsibilities, there can be a tendency to think of her as being exclusively responsible for the student with disabilities, or as being the "teacher" for the student with disabilities. This practice is not appropriate. Paraprofessionals are not certified teachers and should not be expected to function as teachers. Rather, paraprofessionals are employed to assist certified staff in the delivery of educational services to students with and without disabilities. So be certain that you or the special educator take the responsibility to plan instructions for all of the students. Plan carefully how the paraprofessional can assist with the implementation of the instruction.

When there is clarity regarding paraprofessional roles and responsibilities, the classroom teacher maintains primary responsibility for all of the students in the classroom and the paraprofessional assists with this important work. This clarity contributes to a positive working environment.

Quick-Guides to Inclusion: Ideas for Educating Students with Disabilities   ©Michael F. Giangreco
Available through Paul H. Brookes Publishing Co., Baltimore: 1-800-638-3775

#4

Establish Shared Expectations for Student Learning and Classroom Management

---

Quick-Guides to Inclusion: Ideas for Educating Students with Disabilities   ©Michael F. Giangreco
Available through Paul H. Brookes Publishing Co., Baltimore: 1-800-638-3775

Establish Shared Expectations for Student Learning and Classroom Management

As you work with the paraprofessional, keep in mind that the overall goal is student learning. As the classroom teacher, you have an idea of the "big picture" for student learning; it is important that the paraprofessional shares the same expectations. Discuss with him what you hope students will accomplish in the various subjects. Invite him to contribute his thoughts and ideas. Together, develop a set of shared expectations for student learning and classroom management.

Think about the way you manage your classroom. What level of activity are you comfortable with? How do you establish your classroom rules and expectations? What is your typical response to classroom conflicts? Share these thoughts and practices with the paraprofessional. Let him know in which situations he is free to intervene with students, and when he should check with you.

If the paraprofessional has been employed to assist primarily with one student, review the Individualized Education Program (IEP) that has been developed for that student. Explain how the student's IEP goals will be addressed within typical class activities with peers. Show him how he can assist.

When paraprofessionals are left on their own to "figure out" what students are learning and the preferred classroom management system, time may be wasted and misinterpretations made. In addition, students may be given mixed messages regarding the multiple sets of classroom routines that may evolve. When expectations for student learning and classroom management are shared, there is a sense of common purpose for adults and students, as well as clarity regarding what all of the students are learning and how the paraprofessional is expected to support that learning.

Quick-Guides to Inclusion: Ideas for Educating Students with Disabilities   ©Michael F. Giangreco
Available through Paul H. Brookes Publishing Co., Baltimore: 1-800-638-3775

#5

Ensure that
the Paraprofessional Is
Guided by Certified Staff

Ensure that the Paraprofessional
Is Guided by Certified Staff

Always remember that, as the classroom teacher, you are the instructional leader. Even when a paraprofessional has been employed to assist with one or more students, it is your responsibility to oversee the learning environment, including the activities of the paraprofessional. Show the paraprofessional how she can assist in instruction. Remember, typically paraprofessionals are not certified teachers; that is why it can be problematic for paraprofessionals to be given the responsibilities of designing and implementing instruction for students. Often these responsibilities fall to the paraprofessional by default rather than by design. Help the paraprofessional clarify which decisions to make on her own and provide reassurance that she can ask you or the appropriate staff person (e.g., nurse for health-related issues) for assistance.

Consult the team to clarify how the paraprofessional can best support student learning. Make sure the paraprofessional is part of these team discussions. Tell her you are seeking input from the team so that her contributions can be as meaningful as possible.

Too often paraprofessionals are left alone to decide what it is they are supposed to do. When activities are not designed and guided by certified staff, the paraprofessional's efforts can become fragmented and separate from the total learning environment. Classroom practice may be compromised and school policies may be violated unintentionally because the paraprofessional is not part of the formal communication loops.

When certified staff design and guide the activities of paraprofessionals, all students receive a more coordinated and integrated education. Remember, you are the classroom teacher for all of your students, and the paraprofessional is there to assist you.

Quick-Guides to Inclusion: Ideas for Educating Students with Disabilities   ©Michael F. Giangreco
Available through Paul H. Brookes Publishing Co., Baltimore: 1-800-638-3775

#6

Review Paraprofessional Activities Regularly

Review Paraprofessional Activities Regularly

Paraprofessional activities need to be reviewed regularly for appropriateness and effectiveness. When paraprofessionals are providing direct instructional support to students with and without disabilities, they need specific feedback about how well they are doing. Are they providing enough assistance without providing too much? Are they giving students opportunities to learn from mistakes as well as successes? Are their activities and interactions enhancing the total classroom environment?

As the teacher, you can develop a variety of ways to conduct such reviews that become integrated into your daily routine. Ask the paraprofessional to keep a log of how he is using his time, the type of input and training he receives from certified staff, and the like. Review the log with him to see if his daily activities are varied in ways that ensure that he is not supporting the student with disabilities exclusively. If this is happening, develop alternative ways in which the student can be supported (e.g., use of peers, shifting student groupings).

Like anyone else, the paraprofessional's activities should be varied enough that they do not become overly repetitive or mundane. Without some variety, the paraprofessional can lose sight of the overall goal and may devalue his own contributions. With regular reviews, you both will be informed about changes that need to be made before a situation becomes problematic. Such an approach will allow you to put your energies into proactive, rather than reactive, efforts.

Quick-Guides to Inclusion: Ideas for Educating Students with Disabilities ©Michael F. Giangreco
Available through Paul H. Brookes Publishing Co., Baltimore: 1-800-638-3775

#7

Establish Procedures
for Unexpected Situations

Quick-Guides to Inclusion: Ideas for Educating Students with Disabilities   ©Michael F. Giangreco
Available through Paul H. Brookes Publishing Co., Baltimore: 1-800-638-3775

Establish Procedures for Unexpected Situations

Schools are places of continual change. Schedules, absences, field trips, special events, visitors, assemblies, testing days, and myriad other irregularities make absolute consistency impossible. As a classroom teacher, you know the importance of flexibility and probably have strategies to deal with unexpected changes in daily routines. This may not be true for the paraprofessional. As you begin the school year, share with her a copy of the typical daily and weekly schedules. Be certain to provide her with the necessary training and support that she will need in order to facilitate many of the typical daily routines.

Discuss with the paraprofessional how you would like to handle unexpected changes in daily routines. Be as specific as possible. For example, what happens when the teacher, the paraprofessional, or other classroom personnel is absent? Or, how do you proceed when visitors come to the room? How can the paraprofessional be helpful during these times? What are the paraprofessional's responsibilities when students are engaging in testing or field trips? Does the paraprofessional have responsibilities related to the implementation of teacher-developed instruction, and, if so, what does she do when instruction is not planned in advance? Develop a strategy (e.g., notes in your plan book, on her desk) where you can communicate changes as you become aware of them. Agree on ways (e.g., time and places) for her to consult with you if she is uncertain about how to proceed.

When paraprofessionals are unaware of what to do in unanticipated situations, they are left in the position of having to guess. Though you cannot predict all of the situations that may occur, you can give guidance to the paraprofessional as to what things cause changes in the typical schedule and preferred ways of responding. This planning will give the paraprofessional a proactive way to contribute to the classroom.

Quick-Guides to Inclusion: Ideas for Educating Students with Disabilities   ©Michael F. Giangreco
Available through Paul H. Brookes Publishing Co., Baltimore: 1-800-638-3775

#8

Ensure that Paraprofessionals Promote Student Responsibility

Quick-Guides to Inclusion: Ideas for Educating Students with Disabilities   ©Michael F. Giangreco
Available through Paul H. Brookes Publishing Co., Baltimore: 1-800-638-3775

Ensure that Paraprofessionals Promote Student Responsibility

Students learn from taking risks; with that risk taking, there are bound to be both successes and failures. It is crucial that students be allowed to experience both. You and the paraprofessional can create a learning place that is safe enough for those risks and supportive enough for real student growth to occur. Talk with the paraprofessional about your own experiences. Tell him about some students you have assisted in becoming more independent and responsible for their own learning. Share examples of students who have learned from their mistakes. Invite the paraprofessional to do the same.

Convey that you are there to make the classroom a place where the students gain more independence and responsibility throughout the year. Stress the importance of monitoring how much assistance he is giving to students. Teach him to ask questions of himself like, "What am I doing for the student that she can do for herself?" "What does the student need to learn to do next to become more independent?" "When was the last time that the student was able to make a mistake?"

When student responsibility is not emphasized or clarified, it is very easy for the paraprofessional to believe that he is there to ensure that the students are experiencing success 100% of the time. He may rush to keep a student from making an error that actually would have resulted in new learning for the student. Be certain to tell the paraprofessional how he is doing related to this guideline.

Emphasizing student responsibility and talking about your roles in relationship to assisting students without "hovering" will create a common vision for all students in your classroom.

Quick-Guides to Inclusion: Ideas for Educating Students with Disabilities ©Michael F. Giangreco
Available through Paul H. Brookes Publishing Co., Baltimore: 1-800-638-3775

#9

Establish Times
and Ways to Communicate

Establish Times and Ways to Communicate

In order to work effectively with the paraprofessional, it is important to communicate on an ongoing basis using both formal and informal strategies. Develop a system of communication that takes into account **what** you need to communicate about, as well as **how** and **when** that will be done.

Generate a list of topics that you frequently need to communicate about (e.g., upcoming activities, daily lesson plans, development of student adaptations, preparation of instructional materials, contacts with parents). How do you currently communicate about these issues (e.g., verbal, written, not at all)? Is the strategy effective and efficient, or does it need modification? As the classroom teacher, you should develop a simple strategy to ensure that communication takes place. Be certain that you maintain communication with the family of the student with disabilities. For example, develop a classroom calendar that highlights upcoming events, provide the paraprofessional with a daily schedule, give her access to your plan book, and write notes about student adaptations and place the notes in your plan book. Commit to using the strategy for several weeks and then reevaluate the effectiveness. Modify it if necessary.

Identify a time during the day or week when you can meet with the paraprofessional to touch base, plan, and discuss classroom and student-specific issues. It has been our experience that 10 minutes a day can do wonders!

When the communication between the classroom teacher and the paraprofessional is poor, the paraprofessional is unclear about both what she is supposed to do and how it is to be done. As a result, she faces a guessing game that puts her at risk of overlooking potentially important instruction. As the classroom teacher, you have a powerful impact on the discussions that occur in your classroom.

Quick-Guides to Inclusion: Ideas for Educating Students with Disabilities   ©Michael F. Giangreco
Available through Paul H. Brookes Publishing Co., Baltimore: 1-800-638-3775

#10

Evaluate the Effectiveness of the Paraprofessional

Evaluating one's effectiveness in supporting the learning and growth of children and youth is very important. The paraprofessional's roles and responsibilities are related to yours as the classroom teacher; therefore, as you provide feedback to the paraprofessional, you will undoubtedly be evaluating yourself in relationship to him. By the very nature of his job, the paraprofessional must rely on you and other team members for direction, training, and feedback. Refer back to the list of responsibilities that were generated by responding to the suggestions in Guideline #3. Use this list as the framework for providing the paraprofessional with specific feedback on his work. For each item, have him indicate how he is doing and what needs improvement. Do the same related to your own roles and responsibilities. Compare your responses and discuss whether he would benefit from additional modeling or training in a particular area. Use this as an opportunity to gather and document information about the paraprofessional's strengths, as well as areas in which he continues to grow.

Through our experiences, we have learned that when paraprofessionals do not receive feedback, they may draw false conclusions about how they are doing. Without direct and substantive training and feedback, they do not receive the benefit of professional assistance in learning how to be effective assistants in the classroom. When paraprofessionals receive ongoing training and assistance and participate in their own evaluation process, it can promote a sense of well-being and effectiveness.

Quick-Guides to Inclusion: Ideas for Educating Students with Disabilities   ©Michael F. Giangreco
Available through Paul H. Brookes Publishing Co., Baltimore: 1-800-638-3775

Selected References

Doyle, M.B. (1997). *The paraprofessional's guide to the inclusive classroom: Working as a team.* Baltimore: Paul H. Brookes Publishing Co.

Doyle, M.B., York-Barr, J., & Kronberg, R.M. (1996). *Creating inclusive school communities: A staff development series for general and special educators: Module 5. Collaboration: Providing support in the classroom.* Baltimore: Paul H. Brookes Publishing Co.

Giangreco, M.F., Baumgart, D., & Doyle, M.B. (1995). Including students with disabilities in general education classrooms: How it can facilitate teaching and learning. *Intervention in School and Clinic, 30*(5), 273–278.

Giangreco, M.F., Edelman, S.W., Luiselli, T.E., & MacFarland, S.Z.C. (in press). Helping or hovering: Effects of instructional assistant proximity on students with disabilities. *Exceptional Children.*

Kronberg, R.M., York-Barr, J., & Doyle, M.B. (1996). *Creating inclusive school communities: A staff development series for general and special educators: Module 2: Curriculum as everything students learn in school: Creating a classroom community.* Baltimore: Paul H. Brookes Publishing Co.

York, J., Doyle, M.B., & Kronberg, R. (1992). A curricular development process for inclusive classrooms. *Focus on Exceptional Children, 25*(4), 1–16.

York-Barr, J., Doyle, M.B., & Kronberg, R.M. (1996). *Creating inclusive school communities: A staff development series for general and special educators: Module 3a: Curriculum as everything students learn in school: Planning for transitions.* Baltimore: Paul H. Brookes Publishing Co.

Quick-Guide #4

Getting the Most Out of Support Services

Michael F. Giangreco, Susan W. Edelman,
Ruth E. Dennis, Patricia A. Prelock, and Chigee J. Cloninger

Quick-Guides to Inclusion:
Ideas for Educating Students with Disabilities

Michael F. Giangreco, Ph.D.
Series Editor

Dear Teacher,

When a student with disabilities is placed in your class-room, it is not uncommon for him or her to be accompanied by an entourage of support personnel assigned, theoretic-ally, to help the student and help you. The type and number of support service personnel vary widely, but usually the more severe or complex the student's disabilities, the larger and more diverse the group you are likely to encounter. This group may include various combinations of special edu-cators, instructional assistants, related services providers (e.g., physical therapists, psychologists, speech-language pathologists, occupational therapists, vision and hearing specialists), and other consultants.

Assignment of support service staff is undoubtedly well intended, but it doesn't always work smoothly. Merely assigning a group of people to a student's program does not ensure that the impact will be supportive of the student or you, as the primary professional who teaches the student. The 10 guidelines included in this Quick-Guide are offered as a framework for you and your team to think about so that support services are provided in ways that truly are helpful within the context of your classroom. Each guideline is followed by a brief description. At the end you'll find a list of "Selected References" if you wish to pursue more in-depth information. In the meantime, this Quick-Guide should facilitate your first steps in getting the most out of support services.

Good Luck!

Michael, Susan, Ruth, Patty, and Chigee

GUIDELINES-AT-A-GLANCE

1. Become Aware of What Support Service Providers Have to Offer

2. Approach Support Service Staff as Collaborators Rather Than Experts

3. Make Sure Team Members Agree on Expectations and Goals for Students

4. Clarify Your Role as a Team Member and Your Relationship with Other Team Members

5. Be Clear About the Types of Supports You Need and Want

6. Distinguish Between Needing an "Extra Pair of Hands" and More Specialized Help

7. Make Sure Support Service Providers Understand Your Classroom Routines

8. Participate in Scheduling Support Services

9. Have the Team Evaluate the Effectiveness of Support Services for the Student

10. Make Sure Support Services Are Helping You to Do a Better Job

Quick-Guides to Inclusion: Ideas for Educating Students with Disabilities   ©Michael F. Giangreco
Available through Paul H. Brookes Publishing Co., Baltimore: 1-800-638-3775

#1

Become Aware of What Support Service Providers Have to Offer

Become Aware of What
Support Service Providers Have to Offer

As a classroom teacher, you may have had previous experiences working with special education support personnel, or this could be a relatively new experience. In either case, it is important to become knowledgeable about what your team members have to contribute to the team, both professionally and personally. It is equally important for support personnel to learn about the professional and personal skills you bring to the table.

Professionally, we suggest that team members become knowledgeable of each other on two levels. First, it is important to understand the roles of various disciplines, as well as how those roles differ from, and overlap with, other disciplines. For example, what do occupational therapists or orientation and mobility specialists do? How do the activities of these disciplines differ from, or overlap with, other disciplines such as physical therapy or special education? Your knowledge of other disciplines can be increased through face-to-face interactions and by sharing written information. Second, we suggest that team members share their specific professional abilities. For example, the speech-language pathologist on your team may have specialized skills in augmentative communication systems or computer applications, while the psychologist may have a background in nonaversive approaches to dealing with challenging behaviors.

You might be surprised to find out how handy knowledge of personal interests in hobbies, sports, or community activities (gardening, woodworking, music, art, baseball) can be throughout the team process. We suggest you share this information with your team as well. Knowing both the professional and personal knowledge and skills of the various team members should provide a foundation for the team to more fully understand each other and work together.

Quick-Guides to Inclusion: Ideas for Educating Students with Disabilities   ©Michael F. Giangreco
Available through Paul H. Brookes Publishing Co., Baltimore: 1-800-638-3775

#2

Approach
Support Service Staff
as Collaborators
Rather Than Experts

Quick-Guides to Inclusion: Ideas for Educating Students with Disabilities   ©Michael F. Giangreco
Available through Paul H. Brookes Publishing Co., Baltimore: 1-800-638-3775

Approach Support Service Staff as Collaborators Rather Than Experts

We can't expect every team member to have specialized skills in all areas—that's why we need to rely on each other. Working together as a team allows professionals to learn the new skills they will need to obtain training, technical assistance, or consultation from others with specialty skills. If we approach support service personnel as experts, we may inadvertently establish unproductive hierarchies within a team, create unrealistic expectations among team members, and interfere with the very collaboration that is so essential to solving many of the complex challenges presented by students. Yes, many support service personnel have knowledge and skills that are different from yours as a teacher, but don't forget that you also have unique knowledge and skills to bring to the team's efforts. Avoid the "expert" trap by establishing realistic, collaborative expectations among your team members.

Traditional skills associated with particular disciplines and the actual skills of individual team members vary widely, so we cannot assume the nature of the expertise of any team member. We also cannot assume support service personnel have been trained to provide school-based services, given their many subspecialties. For example, a physical therapist may have spent several years working with senior citizens or in a sports medicine clinic and may not necessarily possess the knowledge and skills needed to work with a wide range of children with disabilities.

Even when a professional's focus has been school-based services for children with disabilities, the same issues may exist. For example, a special educator who is trained and accustomed to working with students who have learning disabilities may be asked to support a student who has severe or multiple disabilities (e.g., cognitive, physical, sensory). Therefore, you should strive for collaboration and avoid the "expert" trap.

Quick-Guides to Inclusion: Ideas for Educating Students with Disabilities ©Michael F. Giangreco
Available through Paul H. Brookes Publishing Co., Baltimore: 1-800-638-3775

#3

Make Sure Team Members Agree on Expectations and Goals for Students

---

Quick-Guides to Inclusion: Ideas for Educating Students with Disabilities   ©Michael F. Giangreco
Available through Paul H. Brookes Publishing Co., Baltimore: 1-800-638-3775

Make Sure Team Members Agree on Expectations and Goals for Students

One of the most common sources of anxiety for many general education teachers is grappling with the question, "What am I expected to teach the student with disabilities who is part of my class?" When team members do not share the same expectations about what the student will learn or who should teach her, it can be a source of conflict. It is vital for the classroom teacher to play a substantive and ongoing role in the education of the student with disabilities who receives individually determined support services.

The first step to getting the team on the same wavelength is to reach consensus about the components of the student's educational program. This should include a small set of individualized priority learning outcomes (Individualized Education Program [IEP] goals) and a larger set of additional learning outcomes that reflect the broad curriculum of your class. General supports that are provided for the student should also be determined. Sometimes support service providers suggest having their own set of goals—this should raise a red flag! Separate goals lead to confusion, fragmentation, and disjointed services because team members are moving ahead in different directions rather than agreeing to head in the same direction—a recipe for disaster! Teams must have shared goals!

Once the team has agreed on a student's educational program components, teachers may be realistically anxious about how they will address the student's individualized goals within class activities. Through activity-based experiences, students can pursue individualized goals at appropriate levels in varying curriculum areas. For example, during a social studies board game about world geography, the student with disabilities might be working on geography goals at a different level or may be pursuing learning outcomes from other curriculum areas (e.g., communication, social skills) via the geography activity.

Quick-Guides to Inclusion: Ideas for Educating Students with Disabilities   ©Michael F. Giangreco
Available through Paul H. Brookes Publishing Co., Baltimore: 1-800-638-3775

#4

Clarify Your Role as a Team Member and Your Relationship with Other Team Members

---

Quick-Guides to Inclusion: Ideas for Educating Students with Disabilities   ©Michael F. Giangreco
Available through Paul H. Brookes Publishing Co., Baltimore: 1-800-638-3775

Clarify Your Role as a Team Member and Your Relationship with Other Team Members

As the classroom teacher, you have many responsibilities to all the children in your class. This broadly includes planning, implementing, monitoring, evaluating, and adjusting their instruction. Doing these same things for students in your room who have disabilities is also a vital aspect of your role. Although many general education teachers explain that they are not trained to teach students with disabilities, we have repeatedly seen that the basic principles of teaching and learning are the same, regardless of the labels assigned to children; therefore, with the right kinds of support, a capable teacher can teach any type of student.

Planning for, and supervising, the activities of an instructional assistant is a new responsibility for some teachers. Handing over too much responsibility to an instructional assistant can leave you out of touch with the student with disabilities and can create problems of dependence between the student with disabilities and the instructional assistant. We suggest that the teacher retain primary responsibility for planning instruction. Make sure you have opportunities to teach the student with disabilities so that you will have enough involvement to report on the student's progress thoughtfully.

Here are a few questions to ask yourself. If the answer to any of these questions is "No," then problems are likely to occur.

- Do I plan instruction for the student with disabilities to about the same extent as I do for other students?
- Do I spend as much time teaching the student with disabilities as others in the class?
- Do I spend time with the student with disabilities during noninstructional times?
- Do I play a primary role in evaluating the progress of the student with disabilities?

Quick-Guides to Inclusion: Ideas for Educating Students with Disabilities   ©Michael F. Giangreco
Available through Paul H. Brookes Publishing Co., Baltimore: 1-800-638-3775

#5

Be Clear About
the Types of Supports
You Need and Want

Be Clear About the Types of Supports You Need and Want

A mismatch between what teachers want from support personnel and what they get is a common problem. For example, you want someone to demonstrate a teaching method but instead he hands you an article to read, or you need certain materials and instead you have a meeting. It is important to clarify for yourself and your team the types, content, and intensity of supports you need and want on an ongoing basis. Listed here are four basic types of supports that you may need.

Resource Support includes 1) tangible materials (e.g., adapted equipment), 2) financial resources (e.g., funds for community-based learning), 3) informational resources (e.g., professional literature), and 4) human resources (e.g., parent volunteers, peer tutors).

Moral Support includes interactions that validate the worth of people's efforts, sending the message, "You are headed in a positive direction—keep going." This includes active listening characterized by nonjudgmental acceptance of ideas and feelings. When they are provided moral support, enough trust exists between people so that perspectives can be shared without fear of put-downs, criticism, or breaches in confidentiality.

Technical Support includes concrete strategies, methods, approaches, and ideas. This can be accomplished through in-service training, staff development activities, peer coaching, collaborative consultation, demonstration, modeling, or problem-solving sessions. Technical assistance results in the acquisition of new skills that can be implemented, adjusted, and reimplemented in a cyclical fashion as necessary to meet student and team member needs.

Evaluation Support includes assistance in collecting and presenting information that allows the program and supports for a student with disabilities to be monitored and adjusted. It also provides ways to assess the impact of support services on students, families, and professionals.

Quick-Guides to Inclusion: Ideas for Educating Students with Disabilities   ©Michael F. Giangreco
Available through Paul H. Brookes Publishing Co., Baltimore: 1-800-638-3775

#6

Distinguish Between Needing an "Extra Pair of Hands" and More Specialized Help

---

Quick-Guides to Inclusion: Ideas for Educating Students with Disabilities   ©Michael F. Giangreco
Available through Paul H. Brookes Publishing Co., Baltimore: 1-800-638-3775

Distinguish Between Needing an "Extra Pair of Hands" and More Specialized Help

When teachers need human resources, it is important to distinguish between the need for someone who has specialized skills and the need for someone who can provide an extra pair of helping hands. Making this distinction clearly will help ensure that resources are beneficial and efficient. Sometimes teachers come to rely on support service personnel (e.g., special educators, speech-language pathologists) as an extra pair of helping hands and can feel let down when these support personnel schedule other activities and are not present. If teachers need extra hands, but not necessarily specialized services, we suggest first drawing on natural supports such as classmates, cross-age tutors, parent volunteers, or community members. The next level of human resources may be to hire an instructional assistant for the classroom. Sometimes what teachers really want and need are specialized support personnel to solve problems, suggest adaptations or accommodations, or demonstrate specific strategies.

Consider the following scenarios as examples to help distinguish between the need for an extra pair of hands and the need for specialized support.

- The instructional assistant is absent and the teacher needs someone to help run some planned activities. (helping hands)
- The teacher is having difficulty finding a writing implement that works well for a student with physical disabilities. (specialized support)
- The teacher has planned a field trip to the local science museum and needs assistance supervising the students. (helping hands)
- The teacher is planning a new math unit and is having difficulty figuring out meaningful ways to include the student with disabilities. (specialized support)

Each time you find yourself needing human resources, ask yourself, "Do I need an extra pair of helping hands or specialized support?"

Quick-Guides to Inclusion: Ideas for Educating Students with Disabilities   ©Michael F. Giangreco
Available through Paul H. Brookes Publishing Co., Baltimore: 1-800-638-3775

#7

Make Sure
Support Service Providers
Understand Your
Classroom Routines

Make Sure Support Service Providers Understand Your Classroom Routines

As the only professional staff member in your classroom all the time, no one is in a better position to know the flow of activities and classroom routines better than you—the teacher. Teachers have repeatedly told us that many of the "recommendations" they receive from support service personnel simply won't work in a general education class because support service personnel are not sufficiently aware of the classroom context and dynamics (e.g., cooperative groups, class rules, routines, other students).

Even the most skillful consultant needs to apply her individual skills within the context of the classroom to be most effective. Although we hope that support service personnel will become increasingly aware of the importance of learning and understanding the classroom context and dynamics, this needs to be a primary concern of every teacher who hopes to receive meaningful support.

Consider generating a list that can be posted in your classroom or shared with team members regarding the types of contextual information you think are most critical for people to know. For example, a student approached a support service staff member to ask for the answer to a question on a class assignment. The support service provider thought she was being helpful when she answered the student's question. She didn't know that the teacher had established a protocol for students to first "look it up" and then "ask a classmate" before asking a teacher, who would then guide students to the information rather than simply telling them the answer—so much for good intentions.

What information do you want support service personnel to be aware of in your classroom? Do you prefer that the support staff jump right into activities or be flies on the wall? What class governance rules and routines should they be aware of? Do they know, for example, that every Friday afternoon you have a special science activity? Let the team know.

Quick-Guides to Inclusion: Ideas for Educating Students with Disabilities ©Michael F. Giangreco
Available through Paul H. Brookes Publishing Co., Baltimore: 1-800-638-3775

#8

Participate in
Scheduling Support Services

Teachers sometimes tell us that they feel they are at the mercy of the many support service providers' schedules. The result is that support service providers may show up in the classroom at inopportune times. Sometimes the presence of support service personnel can become downright overwhelming when they arrive in groups, either on purpose or by accident. This potential disruption to the classroom can be avoided with a bit of preplanning.

Although balancing the scheduling needs of many people is always a challenge, we suggest that teachers be proactive about 1) the purpose of the support service provider's visit (e.g., to observe the student's participation in a large-group language arts activity and collaborate on problem-solving ideas for meaningful inclusion), 2) when they want support personnel to be in the classroom (e.g., particular times of day or days of the week), 3) when they want to sit down and meet with support service providers (e.g., during fourth period when the students are in physical education, during recess, or after school), 4) whether or not they want more than one support service person in the room at a time (e.g., overlapping support service personnel may be beneficial/necessary or not), and 5) what actions and follow-up will take place as a result of the visit (e.g., development of an action plan or follow-up activities). Of course, the solutions to these and other scheduling-related problems will undoubtedly be different across situations, requiring individualization and flexibility.

Some classroom teachers prefer to have the student's case manager arrange for the visits of support service providers. Even if this is agreeable to the classroom teacher, all of the aforementioned points are still relevant to consider and act on. Being proactive about scheduling support services can ensure that services are used most efficiently and, we hope, that teachers will find the involvement of service providers increasingly helpful.

Quick-Guides to Inclusion: Ideas for Educating Students with Disabilities ©Michael F. Giangreco
Available through Paul H. Brookes Publishing Co., Baltimore: 1-800-638-3775

#9

Have the Team
Evaluate the Effectiveness
of Support Services
for the Student

Quick-Guides to Inclusion: Ideas for Educating Students with Disabilities ©Michael F. Giangreco
Available through Paul H. Brookes Publishing Co., Baltimore: 1-800-638-3775

Have the Team Evaluate the Effectiveness of Support Services for the Student

Because there are national shortages in many support services (e.g., speech-language pathology, physical therapy), parents and school personnel alike often feel fortunate to have a service available and listed on a student's IEP. We often, however, fail to evaluate whether the service is having the effects we originally intended. Sometimes it is unclear from the IEP just what the intended impact of support services is supposed to be. When this is unclear, related services can become parallel services rather than those "required to assist a student with disabilities to benefit from special education," as stated in the Individuals with Disabilities Education Act of 1990 (PL 101-476). Support services must be **both** educationally relevant and necessary. This is much different from asking, "Can a service help?" The answer to this question will almost always be "Yes." It is not the team's job to provide every conceivable service that might help, but rather to provide those services that are necessary for the student to receive an appropriately individualized education.

Once services are provided, we need to continually evaluate their impact. To adequately evaluate support services, we must know 1) explicitly which parts of the educational program they are intended to support and 2) the kinds of approaches being used to be supportive (e.g., making adaptations, training others). To evaluate these aspects of support services, it is important to ask how the approaches of support personnel are related to the student's educational program and to what extent. Next, we need to ask whether support services have been effective in increasing the student's access to educational opportunities or have had a positive impact on student learning. Finally, and most important, we must consider whether the student's life is better as a result of receiving support services. The team's responses to these and related evaluation questions will provide substantive information to assist with future decisions.

Quick-Guides to Inclusion: Ideas for Educating Students with Disabilities   ©Michael F. Giangreco
Available through Paul H. Brookes Publishing Co., Baltimore: 1-800-638-3775

#10

Make Sure
Support Services
Are Helping You
to Do a Better Job

The bottom line is that support services should be helping teachers do their jobs better and easier. Consider the following Top 10 signs of problems:

Top 10 Signs that You
Do **Not** Find a Consultant's Input Supportive

10. You cancel the consultant's scheduled visit to the classroom because of possible Elvis sightings.

9. When you spot a consultant coming down the hall, you duck into the nearest closet or vacant classroom to avoid being asked to do another task you find irrelevant.

8. When consultants show up in the classroom, you first ignore them and then pretend that they weren't expected.

7. Several minutes into a visit by a consultant you say, "Remind me again why you're here?"

6. You offer to donate your time with the consultant to more "needy" staff members.

5. You keep a do-it-yourself voodoo doll and pins handy, just in case the consultant asks for too much.

4. At the end of a visit by the consultant, you have conveniently left your calendar in another state and therefore have a legitimate excuse for not scheduling a follow-up visit.

3. As soon as the consultant is at least 300 yards off school property, you ignore the consultant's recommendations.

2. The equipment left by the consultant for your use fails the "white glove test" and is submitted to the Guinness Book of World Records in the category "Most Dust Accumulation in a Public School Classroom."

1. You shred written suggestions left by the consultant as bedding for the classroom hamster.

Selected References

England, J. (1994). *Related services in inclusive classrooms.* Detroit: Developmental Disabilities Institute, The University Affiliated Program of Michigan, Wayne State University.

Giangreco, M.F. (1996). *Vermont interdependent services team approach (VISTA): A guide to coordinating educational support services.* Baltimore: Paul H. Brookes Publishing Co.

Giangreco, M.F., Cloninger, C.J., & Iverson, V.S. (1993). *Choosing options and accommodations for children (COACH): A guide to planning inclusive education.* Baltimore: Paul H. Brookes Publishing Co.

Giangreco, M.F., Dennis, R., Edelman, S., & Cloninger, C. (1994). Dressing your IEPs for the general education climate: Analysis of IEP goals and objectives for students with multiple disabilities. *Remedial and Special Education, 15*(5), 288–296.

Giangreco, M.F., Edelman, S., & Dennis, R. (1991). Common professional practices that interfere with the integrated delivery of related services. *Remedial and Special Education, 12*(2), 16–24.

Individuals with Disabilities Education Act of 1990, PL 101-476, 20 U.S.C. § 1400 et seq.

Mar, H. (1991). Retooling psychology to serve children and adolescents with severe disabilities. *School Psychology Review, 20*(4), 510–521.

Rainforth, B., & York-Barr, J. (1997). *Collaborative teams for students with severe disabilities: Integrating therapy and educational services* (2nd ed.). Baltimore: Paul H. Brookes Publishing Co.

York, J., Giangreco, M.F., Vandercook, T., & Macdonald, C. (1992). Integrating support personnel in inclusive classrooms. In S. Stainback & W. Stainback (Eds.), *Curriculum considerations in inclusive classrooms: Facilitating learning for all students* (pp. 101–116). Baltimore: Paul H. Brookes Publishing Co.

Quick-Guide #5

Creating Positive
Behavioral Supports

Barbara J. Ayres and Deborah L. Hedeen

Quick-Guides to Inclusion:
Ideas for Educating Students with Disabilities

Michael F. Giangreco, Ph.D.
Series Editor

Quick-Guides to Inclusion: Ideas for Educating Students with Disabilities   ©Michael F. Giangreco
Available through Paul H. Brookes Publishing Co., Baltimore: 1-800-638-3775

Dear Teacher,

Have you ever used the phrase "I'm at my wits' end!" when referring to a student in your classroom? Is this a student who doesn't seem to pay attention to the rules, destroys the property of others, ignores others' personal space, talks back, and/or doesn't respond to the consequences that have been effective with other students over the years? While these are all difficult behaviors to address in the classroom, the solutions are often quite "low tech" and common sense, and they can be created by concerned adults and students working together.

The purpose of this Quick-Guide on creating positive behavioral supports in the inclusive classroom is to provide you with a number of guidelines that we feel you might find helpful as you work collaboratively with others to address behavioral issues presented by students. Each guideline includes a brief description and examples that help each point come to life. At the end of this Quick-Guide you will find a list of "Selected References" that you can refer to if you are interested in gaining additional information on any of the points presented. We hope the guidelines presented in this Quick-Guide will help you get started with creating positive behavioral supports for students who have difficult behaviors.

Good Luck!

Barb and Deb

GUIDELINES-AT-A-GLANCE

1. Get a Little Help from Your Friends

2. Establish Shared Expectations About the Student's Educational Program

3. Understand Your Posture or Attitude Toward the Student Who Has Difficult Behaviors

4. Consider the Message Behind the Behavior

5. Help the Student Feel a Sense of Control over the Classroom Environment

6. Share Information with the Student's Classmates

7. Focus on the Prevention of Problems

8. Teach New, Positive Skills that Will Help the Student Interact and Communicate

9. Respond in Positive, Supportive Ways When the Student Is Having Difficulty

10. Evaluate Your Teaching and Your Interactions with the Student

Quick-Guides to Inclusion: Ideas for Educating Students with Disabilities   ©Michael F. Giangreco
Available through Paul H. Brookes Publishing Co., Baltimore: 1-800-638-3775

#1

Get a Little Help
from Your Friends

Get a Little Help from Your Friends

Including a student who has difficult behaviors in the general education classroom is not an easy job. As a teacher, your attention needs to go to all of your students, not just one. It is sometimes hard to work alone to solve all of the problems that arise during a typical day! Teachers we have worked with have found it most effective to create a "problem-solving team" that works together to focus on the specific needs of the student. It is best if the members of the team know the student well and can spend some time in the classroom, or watch videotapes of classroom activities, so that everyone has a shared understanding of the issues you face as the classroom teacher. For example, in one school where we worked, the problem-solving team included the classroom teacher and classroom assistant, the child's mother, a speech-language therapist, and a special education consultant.

As a team, you can follow a problem-solving format to start the process of determining what the difficulties are, how you can prevent problems, what new skills need to be taught, and how you can respond in positive ways when problems do arise. Often, it is easier for people who are not directly involved on a day-to-day basis to provide new ideas or help you refocus your energy where it will be most beneficial.

It is also important to consider the child himself as a member of the problem-solving team, as well as classmates. Children can have incredible insights into issues and offer a very different, and often quite refreshing, perspective.

Quick-Guides to Inclusion: Ideas for Educating Students with Disabilities   ©Michael F. Giangreco
Available through Paul H. Brookes Publishing Co., Baltimore: 1-800-638-3775

#2

Establish
Shared Expectations
About the Student's
Educational Program

Establish Shared Expectations About the Student's Educational Program

When using a team approach to problem solving, it is important that all members have a shared vision of the priority educational goals and objectives for the student. When working with a student who has difficult behaviors, it is easy to think of the things you wish the child would not do, yet it is important to determine the positive behaviors you want the child to learn. Goals and objectives for the student's Individualized Education Program (IEP) should be centered around these positive behaviors versus what you want the student to stop doing.

Consider the following goal and objective taken from the IEP of a young girl and ask yourself if they communicate the new skills that the child should learn to replace the difficult behaviors:

Goal: To extinguish negative and/or aggressive behaviors toward self and others.

Objective: Refrain from hitting, kicking, or biting others by removal from group.

We hope your answer is "No." This goal and objective describe what the student should *stop* doing. A positive goal and objective might read as follows:

Goal: To increase ability to transition from one activity to another.

Objective: When given one reminder about the amount of time left before a transition and a picture of the next activity, the student will complete the activity she is engaged in and move to the next within 1 minute of the verbal cue.

When you and your team members have a clear idea of the positive educational needs of the child, and can articulate them in writing through the IEP, you will find that you are making progress toward developing a path you can follow to support a student.

Quick-Guides to Inclusion: Ideas for Educating Students with Disabilities   ©Michael F. Giangreco
Available through Paul H. Brookes Publishing Co., Baltimore: 1-800-638-3775

#3

Understand Your Posture or Attitude Toward the Student Who Has Difficult Behaviors

---

Quick-Guides to Inclusion: Ideas for Educating Students with Disabilities   ©Michael F. Giangreco
Available through Paul H. Brookes Publishing Co., Baltimore: 1-800-638-3775

Understand Your Posture or Attitude
Toward the Student Who Has Difficult Behaviors

At times, a student who has difficult behaviors will push us to our limits and bring out the worst in us! Although it is difficult to remain calm and supportive when a student is "pushing our buttons," it is exactly at that time when we must remain stable and continue to provide positive direction to the student.

There are four different "postures" or "attitudes" that guide how we react in times of crisis. First, we can be **overprotective.** A teacher with this attitude is communicating a message to the student that he can do whatever he would like and that there are no boundaries. Teachers who have this posture often say, "I just don't want to rock the boat." Second, we can be cold and **mechanistic.** With this attitude, the teacher just sticks to the established rewards and consequences and will not bend to accommodate a student and possibly prevent problems from occurring or getting worse. Third, we can have an **authoritarian** attitude. This is when the teacher is the "boss" and the student had better follow the rules or he will be in big trouble! A teacher with this attitude will often rely on negative consequences in an effort to shape a student's behavior. Fourth, we can have an attitude of **respect, relationship, and solidarity** with a student. With this attitude, the teacher communicates a message to the student that "we are in this together." This teacher is flexible and supportive and resolves conflict actively with the student by providing direction and positive support, even during a conflict situation. While we will find it difficult, if not impossible, to always remain calm and supportive, we should strive to develop this attitude as our classroom "umbrella."

Quick-Guides to Inclusion: Ideas for Educating Students with Disabilities   ©Michael F. Giangreco
Available through Paul H. Brookes Publishing Co., Baltimore: 1-800-638-3775

#4

Consider the Message
Behind the Behavior

Consider the Message Behind the Behavior

Although you might feel that the student in your classroom who has difficult behaviors is sometimes deliberately trying to "ruin your day," behaviors usually serve a more specific purpose for the child and make perfect sense to her. Some students have limited language or have learned to use behaviors to "make things happen" in their school or home environments or both. There are a number of different messages that are communicated through the use of behaviors.

First, the student may be using the behavior to tell you that she needs your attention. For example, if a child wants you to come to her right away, what might be the most effective approach—waiting quietly at the desk or pushing over the desk?! Second, a student might want to escape an activity because she is bored or finds it too difficult. If the student repeatedly pushes the materials off the desk, your current response might be to have her take a "time-out," which allows her to effectively get out of the task through the use of her behavior. Third, the behavior might serve a play function. The student might be thinking, "It just feels good to do this behavior, it is entertaining, and I can get a reaction from the adults in the classroom too!" Fourth, the child might use the behavior for self-regulation. That is, the behavior might help the student focus, slow down, or speed up (e.g., rocking, foot tapping).

The goal in identifying the communicative intent of the behavior is to identify alternative positive skills that can be taught to replace the behavior. So, the student who pulls hair or clothing in an effort to get the attention of classmates is actively taught to tap them on the shoulder to initiate an interaction.

Quick-Guides to Inclusion: Ideas for Educating Students with Disabilities   ©Michael F. Giangreco
Available through Paul H. Brookes Publishing Co., Baltimore: 1-800-638-3775

#5

Help the Student Feel
a Sense of Control over
the Classroom Environment

Help the Student Feel a Sense of Control over the Classroom Environment

All children strive to feel a sense of control in their lives. Sometimes the student who has difficult behaviors just goes about getting this control in ways that we find difficult to understand and accept. This is the student who wants what he wants, when he wants it—NOW! As teachers, our first response might be to get firm, restrict privileges, and try to show him who is the "boss." However, teachers who are most successful in working with students who have difficult behaviors have found that, although they need to provide some overall structure and establish clear boundaries and expectations, they can also provide many opportunities for students to feel a sense of control throughout their school day.

Developing this sense of control can be accomplished in a number of ways. First, it is very important to provide opportunities for students to make decisions and provide their input regarding the day's activities. For some students we need to create a balance between what they **have** to do and what they **want** to do by providing opportunities for choice making. This can be facilitated within activities (e.g., what materials) and between activities (e.g., what he wants to do now). Students can also choose with whom they want to engage in activities and where they would like to complete the activity. Second, a teacher can provide a specific schedule for a student so she will know the flow of activities for the day. A personal, concrete schedule is often best when the student puts her day together through words and/or pictures and crosses off activities once they are completed. Third, if activities can be made more concrete (e.g., visual, tactile), the student will often be more successful in remaining "on task." It is helpful when the task itself includes natural cues that signal completion. With some tasks that are less concrete, teachers will need to be creative by building cues into the task that signal when it is finished.

Quick-Guides to Inclusion: Ideas for Educating Students with Disabilities   ©Michael F. Giangreco
Available through Paul H. Brookes Publishing Co., Baltimore: 1-800-638-3775

#6

Share Information with
the Student's Classmates

Share Information with the Student's Classmates

When a student with difficult behaviors is educated in a general education classroom, peers will often observe and question the behavior of the student and the responses of the adults. It is important to recognize that classmates model the attitudes and behaviors of the adults in the setting. Although we have always been concerned with confidentiality of students receiving special education services, the fact that we do not say anything about a child's behavior does not mean that other students do not see it occurring. We feel it is important to talk honestly with classmates so they can begin to understand why the student is using certain behaviors.

A first-grade teacher we know talked to her students about what they thought their classmate might be trying to communicate to them when he got upset. One student said, "At the beginning of the year Sean's screams were just screams to us. But now, we can tell if they mean frustration, happiness, sadness, fright, or if he just wants us to leave him alone. Sometimes we have to change some activities so he can participate. But, however he lives, or however he talks to us, he is still one of us."

Another teacher discussed similarities and differences that exist among all people and had the students identify these qualities in themselves. He then read stories about students with disabilities. One day when the student with difficult behaviors was out of the classroom, the teacher facilitated a discussion about how they could tell when he was becoming upset and what they could do to redirect his attention to something else in an effort to prevent problems from occurring. The students generated a list of ideas and picked two they would try during the next few weeks. Students are much more supportive of their classmates when they are given accurate information and an invitation to problem-solve with adults.

Quick-Guides to Inclusion: Ideas for Educating Students with Disabilities   ©Michael F. Giangreco
Available through Paul H. Brookes Publishing Co., Baltimore: 1-800-638-3775

#7

Focus on the
Prevention of Problems

The most effective way to deal with difficult behaviors is to prevent them from ever occurring. The key to prevention is prediction. If you can predict with some degree of accuracy when a challenging behavior is most and least likely to occur, and why, you will be more likely to create environmental changes that will minimize the likelihood of occurrence.

There are at least three ways to think about environmental changes in your classroom. First, you can think about changing the **physical environment.** For example, each morning Jane walked by the teacher's desk and knocked her pencil container and books off onto the floor. So, the teacher created an alternate walking route so Jane no longer passed by her desk.

Second, you can adapt the **instructional environment** by changing the amount of work you are requiring from the student, or by using different materials. Asking questions like, "Is this work too hard, or too easy?" can help you make necessary modifications that will allow the student to be successful.

Third, the **social environment** involves changing how and when people interact with each other. In one classroom, students were asked to sit next to their partners to complete an assignment. One student would hit her partner in order to get his attention. Placing the student across from her partner encouraged the student to use her voice to get his attention. There are many ways to change the environment so that students will be more successful.

Quick-Guides to Inclusion: Ideas for Educating Students with Disabilities   ©Michael F. Giangreco
Available through Paul H. Brookes Publishing Co., Baltimore: 1-800-638-3775

#8

Teach New, Positive Skills that Will Help the Student Interact and Communicate

---

Teach New, Positive Skills that Will Help the Student Interact and Communicate

Many successful teachers work to prevent problems while actively teaching new skills. For some students, the inability to effectively communicate their thoughts or feelings will cause them to use other forms of behavior in order to get their needs met. These behaviors may include hitting, swearing, throwing objects, or refusing to participate. The reason students use these behaviors is because they are often effective ways to accomplish their goals. So, our job is to teach new, more acceptable ways to communicate the same message.

You will want to ask yourself, "How can I teach the student to communicate in a more positive way instead of using the behavior?" Once you select an alternative skill for the student to learn, then that is the skill to teach. For example, one student often pinched the teacher during reading group. The student had learned that "If I pinch, the teacher will remove me from the group and I will not have to work." Once the teacher realized that the student did not know another way to ask to leave the group, she decided to actively teach this new skill by presenting a card that said "break" and assisting him to point to it and take a short break at regular intervals during reading group.

The student may not respond immediately to your new teaching strategies. Continuous modeling and active teaching of new skills will show the student that there are more effective ways to communicate and interact with others. Your positive interactions with the student will encourage successful participation over time.

Quick-Guides to Inclusion: Ideas for Educating Students with Disabilities   ©Michael F. Giangreco
Available through Paul H. Brookes Publishing Co., Baltimore: 1-800-638-3775

#9

Respond in Positive, Supportive Ways When the Student Is Having Difficulty

---

Quick-Guides to Inclusion: Ideas for Educating Students with Disabilities   ©Michael F. Giangreco
Available through Paul H. Brookes Publishing Co., Baltimore: 1-800-638-3775

Respond in Positive, Supportive Ways When the Student Is Having Difficulty

Do you find yourself asking, "But what should I do when she...?" Although it is tempting to spend your time trying to figure out what to do after a behavior has occurred, we believe it is through prevention and teaching that you can most effectively create change in a student's behavior.

However, there will be times when a student will display behaviors that you cannot prevent. It will be important that you support the student during the difficult times so that no one is harmed and the environment is restored while allowing all participants to maintain a reasonable degree of dignity. Discussing or addressing the student's behavior while everyone is frustrated and exhausted is usually not the best solution.

An alternative idea is to think of quick, creative ways to engage the student in the activity at hand so that you can continue teaching. If the student has chosen to go to a different place in the room, then take the materials to the student so that he can continue working. If the student is refusing to work, then provide some choices so that he can select one thing to do. If the student is starting to tire, then let the student know how much work is left before taking a break.

There is an element of give and take—of negotiation—in helping to solve a challenging situation. It is not merely an attempt to control another person, but rather to understand and reach a mutually acceptable solution.

Quick-Guides to Inclusion: Ideas for Educating Students with Disabilities   ©Michael F. Giangreco
Available through Paul H. Brookes Publishing Co., Baltimore: 1-800-638-3775

#10

Evaluate Your Teaching and Your Interactions with the Student

---

Evaluate Your Teaching and Your Interactions with the Student

Creating positive behavioral supports is an ongoing process that requires constant attention and reevaluation. Although we used to take a more simplistic view of behavior change, we now recognize that it is a complex process that requires concentrated effort by a team of people over time. By developing behavioral support plans that address prevention, teaching, and responding, we are initially making our "best guess" as to what might be effective. These best guesses will need to be refined as we learn more about the student and the purpose of his behavior.

One tool that can be extremely effective in the evaluation process is the use of videotapes of the student in the classroom. By capturing segments of the student's day on videotape, you can assess the areas that have been described in this Quick-Guide, such as your posture or attitude toward the student, the message behind the behavior, prevention strategies, new skills that need to be addressed, and responding to the student in positive, supportive ways. Asking others to view and critique the videotaped footage with you is an excellent way to get feedback and direction.

In the absence of videotape equipment, requesting that team members observe within the classroom during difficult times, and during successful times, will help you gather necessary information that will allow you to modify your plans.

You and your team members must recognize and value the ongoing process of evaluation and be willing to reconsider your intervention support plan to make the necessary changes that will allow the student, and the adults, to achieve success.

Selected References

Ayres, B.J., & Hedeen, D.L. (1996). Been there, done that, didn't work: Alternative solutions for behavior problems. *Educational Leadership, 53*(5), 48–50.

Evans, I.M., & Meyer, L.H. (1985). *An educative approach to behavior problems: A practical decision model for interventions with severely handicapped learners.* Baltimore: Paul H. Brookes Publishing Co.

Hedeen, D.L. Ayres, B.J., Meyer, L.H., & Waite, J. (1996). Quality inclusive schooling for students with severe behavioral challenges. In D.H. Lehr & F. Brown (Eds.), *People with disabilities who challenge the system* (pp. 127–171). Baltimore: Paul H. Brookes Publishing Co.

Janney, R., Black, J., & Ferlo, M. (1989). *A problem-solving approach to challenging behaviors.* Syracuse, NY: Syracuse University, Special Projects.

Koegel, L.K., Koegel, R.L., & Dunlap, G. (Eds.). (1996). *Positive behavioral support: Including people with difficult behaviors in the community.* Baltimore: Paul H. Brookes Publishing Co.

Lovett, H. (1996). *Learning to listen.* Baltimore: Paul H. Brookes Publishing Co.

Reichle, J., & Wacker, D.P. (Eds.). (1993). *Communicative alternatives to challenging behavior: Integrating functional assessment and intervention strategies.* Baltimore: Paul H. Brookes Publishing Co.

Topper, K., Williams, W., Leo, K., Hamilton, R., & Fox, T. (1994). *A positive approach to understanding and addressing challenging behaviors.* Burlington: University of Vermont, University Affiliated Program of Vermont.

Quick-Guides to Inclusion: Ideas for Educating Students with Disabilities   ©Michael F. Giangreco
Available through Paul H. Brookes Publishing Co., Baltimore: 1-800-638-3775

Practical and easy to use . . .
More tools to help you include all students.

Choosing Outcomes and Accommodations for Children (COACH)

A Guide to Educational Planning for Students with Disabilities

Second Edition

By **Michael F. Giangreco, Ph.D., Chigee J. Cloninger, Ph.D.,** & **Virginia Salce Iverson, M.Ed.**

This manual provides a practical assessment and planning process for the inclusion of students with disabilities in general education classrooms. Features new to this second edition include a preparation checklist to familiarize participants with the COACH system, a question-and-answer section designed to enhance communication between parents and professionals, and improved forms for planning and evaluating student programs. With this user-friendly tool, educational teams will be able to identify the content of students' educational programs, incorporate programs into a general education setting, and pursue family-valued outcomes.

Stock #3238/Giangreco/COACH 2nd edition/approx. $33.95/1998/approx. 224 pages/8$\frac{1}{2}$ x 11/spiral-bound/ISBN 1-555766-323-8

Vermont Interdependent Services Team Approach (VISTA)

A Guide to Coordinating Educational Support Services

By **Michael F. Giangreco, Ph.D.**

This field-tested manual enables IEP team members to fulfill the related services provisions of IDEA as they make effective support services decisions using a collaborative team approach. Ten specific guidelines set forth a problem-solving process that involves families and leads to greater opportunities for students with mild to severe disabilities. Real-life examples and reproducible forms enhance the usefulness of this book. Educators, related services providers, and family members will welcome this complement to the COACH manual.

Stock #2304/Giangreco/VISTA/$27.95/1996/176 pages/8$\frac{1}{2}$ x 11/spiral-bound/ISBN 1-555766-230-4

PLACE YOUR ORDER NOW!   FREE shipping and handling on prepaid check orders.

Please send me _____ copy(ies) of **COACH**/Stock #3238/approx. $33.95

Please send me _____ copy(ies) of **VISTA**/Stock #2304/$27.95

___ Bill my institution (purchase order must be attached)   ___ Payment enclosed (make checks payable to Brookes Publishing Co.)

___ VISA   ___ MasterCard   ___ American Express   Credit Card #: _____ Exp. date: _____

Signature: _____   Daytime telephone: _____

Name: _____

Address: _____

City/State/ZIP: _____

Maryland orders add 5% sales tax. Yours to review 30 days risk free. Prices subject to change without notice. Prices may be higher outside the United States.

Photocopy this form and mail or fax it to Brookes Publishing Co., P.O. Box 10624, Baltimore, MD 21285-0624, FAX (410) 337-8539. Or call toll-free (8 A.M.–6 P.M. ET) 1-800-638-3775. Or e-mail custserv@pbrookes.com.